— Notorious —
Memphis Gangster
Diggs Nolen

— NOTORIOUS —
MEMPHIS GANGSTER
DIGGS NOLEN

PATRICK O'DANIEL

THE
History
PRESS

Published by The History Press
Charleston, SC
www.historypress.com

Copyright © 2023 by Patrick O'Daniel
All rights reserved

First published 2023

Manufactured in the United States

ISBN 9781467155243

Library of Congress Control Number: 2023938441

Notice: The information in this book is true and complete to the best of our knowledge. It is offered without guarantee on the part of the author or The History Press. The author and The History Press disclaim all liability in connection with the use of this book.

CONTENTS

CONTENTS

ACKNOWLEDGEMENTS

I would like to thank G. Wayne Dowdy, Gina Cordell, Scott Lillard and the staff of the History Department of the Memphis Public Library and Information Center for your support and assistance. I would also like to thank all my friends and family for their love and support—especially Kathy and Kelly, to whom I dedicate this book.

INTRODUCTION

It isn't about what's wrong with you; it's about what happened to you.
—Unknown

MEMPHIS, AUGUST 1928

Diggs Nolen woke up in a jail cell. It was hot and humid in a way that anyone who had never been to Memphis in late August would not believe possible anywhere outside a Southeast Asian jungle. To make matters worse, Diggs had a hangover and a terrible headache—the kind that makes you feel like you are going to die.[1]

Waking up in jail was nothing new for Diggs, but the circumstances that led to his arrest were unusual even for Diggs's standards. Ernest Nolen swore out an insanity warrant against his younger brother the day before and requested the police come to his house and take Diggs into custody. Diggs had been on a monthlong bender and refused to stop drinking. His behavior had become so erratic that his devoted brother worried Diggs had lost his mind.

A jailer came to Diggs's cell and led him down the hall to meet with the police physician. Diggs, who turned forty-one only a week earlier, was about five foot, eight inches tall. He was a handsome man with a slight build, dark hair and dark eyes. Under normal circumstances, Diggs was polished, polite and personable. Convincing the doctor he was right in the head should have been easy for the smooth-talking con man. Today, however, was not normal. Today, Diggs was a disheveled wreck.

Dr. Neumon Taylor, like most Memphians, knew Diggs's turbulent history. He'd read and heard about the college-educated pharmacist who joined a band of bank robbers, participated in one of the biggest heists in New York City, became a narcotics kingpin and led the biggest jailbreak in the county's history. Diggs's mischief, substance abuse and frequent arrests cemented his reputation as an eccentric troublemaker. Reporters wrote about Diggs so often that Diggs joked the only reason anyone bought a newspaper in Memphis was to read about him.[2]

Taylor completed his examination and conferred with Ernest. Given his patient's current state and record of misbehavior, the doctor suggested that a month or two in a secluded insane asylum would do Diggs good. Diggs was incensed. "It's all a lot of bunk," he claimed. Diggs argued, but Taylor had made up his mind. The doctor scheduled a lunacy hearing for the following day. Diggs Nolen, one of the city's cleverest and most notorious criminals, now had to go before a judge and prove his sanity. As the jailer led him away, Diggs yelled, "You're crazy if you think I'm crazy!"[3]

Diggs put on a brave face, but all the while, he worried that perhaps the doctor was right. Before his latest arrest, Diggs confided in his brother that he believed something was wrong with his mind. Even so, Diggs had no intention of letting anyone send him away. He knew he would need to put on a stellar performance in court to avoid a trip to the insane asylum. And that would not be easy, given his past.[4]

WE HOLD THE OUTLAW in special regard, whether it is the "noble bandit" we think pursues freedom and heroism, the trickster who makes a fool of law enforcement or the rebel against authority. We glamorize the criminal in movies, music and popular culture and then assuage our inner moral voice by condemning his or her actions as an afterthought. We barely notice the downtrodden soul driven to crime out of desperation, but the outlaw who consciously flouts society's mores for no other reason than the thrill of doing it wins our applause. It is not just any reckless lawbreaker who earns a place on our pedestal, but rather, it is the one who stylishly violates the law we idolize and secretly fantasize about becoming.[5]

Henry Diggs Nolen started life with a bright future. He was born on August 23, 1887, in the village of Tomnolen, Mississippi, to a well-respected family. He was an intelligent and charming boy who loved to read as much as he loved being outdoors. The course of his life changed when an older cousin, Frank Holloway, returned home telling stories of his adventures as an outlaw. Diggs fell under Holloway's spell. In time, Diggs thought it reasonable and necessary, as well as likely to advance of his reputation, that he should become an outlaw like his cousin and wander through the world in pursuit of adventure.

Diggs sometimes played the part of the malicious con man, thief and drug dealer. Other times, he played the charismatic trickster, both cunning and foolish, who defied conventional behavior and playfully disrupted everyday life. Diggs achieved the celebrity status he so desired, but underneath his devil-may-care attitude lay a deeply conflicted man torn apart by his thirst for excitement and desire for respectability. His story brings to light the crimes he committed in his quixotic quest and the price he paid for living out his childhood fantasy.

Chapter 1

THE FIRE

Power does not corrupt. Fear corrupts…perhaps the fear of a loss of power.
—John Steinbeck

Memphis, March 1899

Diggs Nolen woke up coughing. The groggy twelve-year-old opened his eyes and saw an orange glow in his bedroom. The wooden structure around him sizzled and popped as acrid smoke filled the air. Diggs's heart pounded, and his eyes filled with tears as flames ate away at his walls.

Earlier in the evening, a small fire started when a curtain fell too close to a heating grate. Ella Nolen called the fire department after her son Diggs discovered the fire around eight o'clock. The residents of the boardinghouse at 104 Court Street grumbled when the firemen ordered everyone out. It was hardly an emergency. Mrs. McMillan laughed at Lilly Chapman's wisecracks. Lilly quipped as she made her way downstairs with her children that she would never live on the fourth floor again if she survived the disaster. The firemen put out the tiny flame, and the residents came back inside, sure the danger had passed.

As the boarders settled in for the night, an unnoticed ember from the blaze sparked another fire. Flames spread through the unoccupied first floor, growing in strength as they worked their way up the walls. No one noticed the new fire until they woke around two-thirty in the morning to an inferno in every part of the four-story house.

Memphis Fire Department, circa 1900. *Courtesy of Memphis Public Library and Information Center.*

Some braved the burning stairwell, while others jumped from windows. Dressed in singed bedclothes and coughing from the smoke, they made their way outside into the cool March air. Diggs and his mother, Ella, noticed some of the boarders missing from the group. Where was Katie Lloyd? Where were Lilly and her children? Thomas Bull also saw that not everyone made it out, so the sixty-year-old ran back into the inferno to rescue them.[6]

The firefighters rushed from the Central Fire Station and arrived just as the residents spilled out of the main hall. The blaze lit up the neighborhood, and the house looked like it would collapse. The firefighters forgot their ladders in their rush, so the men had to cut a path through the flames with the spray from their hoses. It took twenty minutes just to make it to the second floor.[7]

Katie Lloyd, the stenographer for Mayor J.J. Williams, woke and found her room full of smoke and her bed on fire. Struggling to breathe, she forced her third-floor window open. The rush of fresh air she wanted so badly only added fuel to the fire. She crawled onto the windowsill to get away from the flames. As she balanced on the narrow ledge, Katie saw her brother Paul Martin leap from a nearby window. She mustered her courage and jumped. Katie fell over twenty feet, slammed into the ground and lay in the alley only feet from the burning house, too stunned to get up.[8]

The smoke cleared as the firemen sprayed the last flames on the fourth floor. It was only then that they noticed the bodies in the front room. Lilly Chapin had led her sons Roy, age ten, and Chester, age four, to the stairwell, only to be cut off by the fire. George Campbell begged Lilly to follow him as he jumped from a window, but Lilly was too scared. Instead, she and her boys huddled together on the bed and waited for the end. All three died from smoke inhalation. Mr. Bull never made it to the Chapins; he collapsed on the second floor and suffocated.[9]

Diggs Nolen recovered from his injuries as news of the tragedy spread around the country. He and the other injured survivors arrived at St. Joseph's Hospital, where doctors treated them for burns, broken bones and shock. On March 25, 1899, newspapers ran the story of the fire and the deaths. Stories with headlines like "Fire Takes More Lives" and "More Deaths in the Flames" horrified readers.[10]

Such an event can leave psychological scars for life. Diggs's parents offered comfort as he coped with the trauma; however, the frightened boy wanted a different kind of solace. He preferred the company of someone larger than life—a person who did not hide from fear but instead sought out and laughed in the face of danger. He wanted a hero.

Chapter 2
FRANK HOLLOWAY

If everybody was satisfied with himself, there would be no heroes.
—Mark Twain

CHICAGO, JANUARY 1912

"My mind is relieved now. I'm ready to hang like a man," drawled Frank Holloway as he lit another cigarette. Inspector Nicholas Hunt had spent the last several hours in the smoky interrogation room listening to Holloway's confession. The veteran detective had heard some far-fetched stories in his life, but nothing like this. Hunt sensed Holloway was up to something, but what could it be?

The previous night, Holloway had roamed the streets of Chicago looking for wallets to steal, but the icy winds had driven most people indoors by sunset. The Mississippian's hands and face had gone numb when he heard the bells and squealing brakes of a southbound Halsted streetcar. Passengers boarded and exited from the doors at either end of the red-and-yellow electric trolley. Holloway worked best in crowds, so he climbed on and squeezed in between the other riders. The passengers shoved their hands in their pockets and tightly cinched their heavy coats. Picking a pocket would prove difficult, so Holloway had to choose his mark carefully.[11]

Holloway was discretely sizing up each passenger when he noticed two men watching him. Most people would not have looked twice at Holloway.

Frank Holloway, Memphis Police Department mug shot, circa 1912. *Courtesy of Memphis Public Library and Information Center.*

He was an unremarkable thirty-two-year-old about five foot, seven inches in height with a medium build, pointed features, dark eyes and a sallow complexion. However, Detectives Lawrence Howe and Thomas O'Malley were not like most people. They knew how to spot a pickpocket.[12]

Holloway, on the other hand, knew how to spot a cop. He moved behind some passengers to avoid the detectives' gaze. He hoped to hide long enough to make a quick escape with the exiting crowd, but the move did not fool the detectives. They grabbed Holloway and pulled him off at the next stop. "All right, take me in," said Holloway after a brief struggle. As the detectives led him away, Holloway added, "It's lucky for you cops I didn't have my two revolvers."[13]

Holloway claimed to be a dangerous criminal and man of many aliases. It seemed more like boasting than remorse, but Inspector Hunt let the man talk. "I'm what they call a bad guy—a real burglar and bank robber. I'm almost anything you want to call me." Hunt listened as Holloway began his extraordinary story.[14]

Holloway was born in 1879 near Winona, Mississippi, the youngest son of attorney Robert Franklin Holloway and Susan Nolen Holloway. He joined Company A of the Second Volunteer Mississippi Regiment in May 1898 and fought in Cuba during the Spanish-American War. After the war, the self-described black sheep of the family left home in search of adventure in the last days of the old Wild West.[15]

Holloway lived his life like a villain from a western novel. He moved from town to town, often with the police, outraged victims or double-crossed accomplices on his trail. Holloway's typical modus operandi was to befriend leading citizens in each new town he visited and set up saloons or hotels as covers for illegal activities such as train robberies, breaking into banks and fraud.[16]

Holloway repeatedly dodged jail time. He claimed self-defense after shooting a comrade during a disagreement over money in St. Louis in 1904. A jury failed to convict him in 1907 for swindling a leading Kansas City citizen. In Tulsa in June 1908, Holloway shot and killed Ed Starr, of the notorious clan that included Belle Starr, during an argument over money. Police released him after he claimed self-defense. Holloway briefly ran a hotel and gambling den in Memphis until police raided the place and ran him out of town. After a quick exit from Memphis, he landed in Claremore, Oklahoma, forming another gang of bank robbers.[17]

Police arrested the gang in April 1910 after they robbed a bank in Harrold, Texas. While out on a $13,000 bond, Holloway set up a meeting with one of his crew in Oklahoma City to discuss dividing their stolen money. As Holloway stepped from his car, the man shot him. Holloway returned fire and wounded him. At the hospital, the injured Holloway refused to name the shooter but promised to get even with him. Left unattended, Holloway snuck out a window and fled the state.[18]

Holloway's story, though embellished, remained believable to the inspector up to this point; however, his tale became more dubious as he continued. Holloway claimed he left for Panama in early 1910, where he and his six cohorts tunneled under the Bank of Panama, broke in and used dynamite to blow open the safe. They made off with the money in a boat with the bank guards in pursuit. Under a hail of gunfire, Holloway evaded the gunboats by detouring into a swamp.[19]

Holloway recounted, "After the robbery, which got the Panama officials and gunboats after us, we went to Colombia and a fight over the division of the money started. One of the fellows named McGuire got three of the fellows siding with him and they started in to shoot at myself and two pals. In the shooting, I croaked a big fellow named Eddie Schaeffer. It was a case of crook get crook; it wasn't murder."

Holloway and the two surviving bandits continued through the jungle. "Ed West and another fellow were in the mix-up," said Holloway. "West, myself and another pal whose name I will not give, started into the jungle to get away from the officials." Holloway killed West in Bogotá after the two bickered over the money. Holloway and his last comrade continued to the coast and returned to the United States.[20]

Holloway made his most outrageous claim when he told Hunt that before the Panama job, he robbed the Bank of Montreal, in New Westminster, Ontario, of $459,000 in September 1911. In thieves' parlance, Holloway said that he "used the soup," or blew the safe. Asked if he was worried about his fate, Holloway leaned back in his chair, took a drag off his cigarette and said, "Why, say boys, I've got $54,000 in a downtown hotel. This stuff [the pickpocketing charge] isn't going to bother me much. I'll get out of it all right."[21]

It seemed unlikely that Holloway would be stealing wallets if he had $54,000 dollars hidden away, but Hunt sent some detectives to search local hotels for the money just in case the story was true. "Holloway may be putting it over on me," said Hunt, "but I am going to find out what truth there is in his story before I lose sight of him. The Tulsa killing is real enough; I guess that is sufficient to warrant detaining him."[22]

At Hunt's request, Assistant Superintendent Edward J. Weiss of the Pinkerton Detective Agency interrogated Holloway. Police had just captured the real mastermind behind the Canadian bank robbery; however, the information had not made the news. Weiss carefully asked questions without giving away new information.

Holloway's timeline did not match the details of the robberies. For example, Holloway claimed the tunnel in Panama took two months to dig. Of course, this was impossible, since it meant the Canadian robbery would have taken place while he was digging the tunnel under the Panamanian bank. Also, Holloway did not know John J. McNamara, the recently captured mastermind behind the Bank of Montreal robbery. Weiss had heard from detectives in Seattle who said that Holloway recently told them the same story before slipping away from them. Weiss confirmed what Hunt suspected; Holloway was lying about the Bank of Montreal. But why?[23]

Holloway's confession appeared to be nothing more than a second-rate crook's attempt at fame, but Weiss had another theory. The Pinkerton detective believed Holloway concocted the stories about the robberies to escape the United States. Holloway was willing to go to Canada but preferred Panama because of the warmer weather. "He has a long record all right and used to be known as a clever crook," said Weiss, "but he never had anything to do with the big jobs he mentioned." Weiss believed Holloway hoped authorities would extradite him to Panama so he could avoid jail time in Texas for the one robbery he truly committed. Once he proved he could not have committed the robbery in Panama, Holloway would be released and out of reach of U.S. law enforcement.[24]

Holloway's plan to escape the country went awry thanks to Weiss. Governor Oscar Colquitt made a formal request for Holloway's return to Texas, and Sheriff J.D. Key arrived a week later and took him back to Wilbarger County to face trial. The jury found Holloway guilty for his part in the Harrold bank robbery.[25]

The wily outlaw, however, proved difficult to hold. In February, Holloway arrived at the state penitentiary at Rusk, a town about ninety miles north of Huntsville in East Texas. A brick wall, twenty feet high and thirty inches deep, enclosed the seven-acre site; however, the prison ran various manufacturing shops and farms beyond the penitentiary confines.[26]

In early August 1912, Holloway was laboring on work detail just outside the walls. He watched the guards and waited for the moment when their attention would wander. When they looked away, he bolted and was long gone before anyone noticed. The alarm eventually sounded, and the posse took off in pursuit, but it was too late. Holloway had too much of a head start, and the posse lost him in the wilds of eastern Texas.

Holloway was now a wanted man. Governor Colquitt offered a $2,000 reward for his capture, so Holloway needed a safe haven quickly. He knew he would not find shelter in Texas or Oklahoma, so he decided to go back to Memphis to lay low for a while. Holloway had cousins there who would take care of him. Perhaps, after a few months in hiding, Holloway thought he might even find some new opportunities in the Bluff City.

Chapter 3
RESCUE

It is the bungled crime that brings remorse.
—P.G. Wodehouse, Love Among the Chickens

SAVANNAH, GEORGIA, NOVEMBER 1912

Diggs Nolen struggled to keep up with the marshal. The officer pulled Diggs's arm to hurry him across the busy train station. The other two marshals kept their hands near their pistols as they studied the faces in the crowd. The train hissed, the conductor shouted and the passengers shuffled through the steam. The lawmen and their quarry stepped aboard.

Diggs dropped into his seat. His eyes focused on his manacled hands in his lap. For an instant, he glanced through the window, and his eyes met a familiar face. Diggs dropped his eyes again so he would not tip off his guards. His escape depended on the element of surprise. He knew Frank Holloway and his friends would gamble their freedom and their lives to keep him from going to prison. They would risk almost anything for a pal. After all, loyalty was part of the outlaw code.

Most American boys of the early twentieth century found heroes in dime novels or Westerns from the silent era of film, but the Nolen, Mitchell and Brantley boys had one of their own. Their cousin Frank Holloway was the most exciting man to come from Tomnolen, Mississippi. What he lacked in size, he more than made up with brashness and personality. Holloway would regale his young cousins on his visits home with his swashbuckling tales of banditry and gunplay. Holloway enjoyed the role as much as the boys loved to hear his stories.[27]

Diggs wanted to become the man Holloway claimed to be more than anything else. Every story Holloway told made Diggs crave the outlaw life more. He dreamed of pursuing adventure, confronting danger and acquiring fame and renown.

Following Frank Holloway on one of his reckless crime sprees was the last thing Diggs's parents wanted him to do. James and Ella Brantley Nolen wanted their son to go to college and become a pharmacist. Ella moved to Memphis so that Diggs could attend preparatory school while James maintained his property in Tomnolen.

Diggs performed well in school, but even his academic success could not break Holloway's spell. At seventeen, Diggs got into a fight with a young man named Charlie Mansell at a bowling alley in Greenville, Mississippi. A deputy broke up the fight and arrested Mansell, but Diggs held a grudge. Like so many other southerners, Diggs had the habit of settling personal matters with firearms as a matter of honor. He ambushed, shot and wounded Mansell after the deputy released him that evening. Diggs later attended Tulane University but was expelled because of a prank. He completed his degree at the College of Physicians and Surgeons in Memphis shortly before it became part of the University of Tennessee.[28]

Diggs spent his summers between semesters, when not getting into trouble, working as a cub reporter under the direction of C.P.J. Mooney. The veteran newspaper editor saw great potential in the restless young man. He said, "I never had about me a brighter, a more accommodating, or pleasant-mannered young fellow than Diggs Nolen when he worked on the paper years ago." Diggs remembered, "[Mooney] was the most righteous man I ever knew. He found the good in me that is hidden generally by the bad that was."[29]

Running a pharmacy seemed dull, so following graduation, Diggs joined his cousins in the Holloway Gang. The gang specialized in confidence scams and cashed bad checks at local banks. Diggs was cautious, but not enough to avoid a careful teller who discovered one of his forged checks at the Union Planters Bank in Memphis in January 1911. Diggs fled the city, but the bank owners hired the Pinkerton Detective Agency to track him down.[30]

Diggs headed west and continued his check schemes, including a forgery at the B.B. Mellon Bank in Temple, Texas. Diggs employed what police called the "biograph method." Following Holloway's example, Diggs would trick a

C.P.J. Mooney, managing editor of the *Commercial Appeal. Courtesy of Memphis Public Library and Information Center.*

well-to-do businessman into signing an innocent document or receipt. Unknown to the man signing his name, Diggs would place a piece of carbon paper under the document and over a forged check. By signing his signature to the first piece of paper, the man unknowingly would also sign his name to the check made out to Diggs. Diggs would then cash the check and quickly leave town.[31]

Under the alias H.K. George, Diggs approached Tom Dennison about cashing a check in the summer of 1911 in Omaha, Nebraska. Diggs explained that he recently sold some real estate in Oklahoma to a man named W.R. Miller and he needed an endorsement to cash the check for $1,980. Dennison offered to help and signed Diggs's draft from the Greenfield State Bank. Diggs used the biograph trick, cashed the check Dennison unknowingly signed and left town.[32]

Diggs underestimated the reach and tenacity of Dennison. The man Diggs thought an easy mark turned out to be a powerful political boss. Dennison pressed charges when he found out about the forged check. Diggs faced additional federal charges because the check had passed through the mail. Dennison also called in favors from his extensive network of friends and political allies to help locate Diggs.[33]

Local detectives, at the request of federal agents, arrested Diggs at his cigar store in Savannah, Georgia, on November 15, 1912. Diggs, who used the alias George W. Thomas, had opened the store after leaving Omaha. His father, James Nolen, under the alias J.T. Thomas, and another cohort named Mr. Green helped run the shop. Police arrested the three but released Green and Nolen's father. Green left town, while the elder Nolen stayed with orders not to discuss the case.[34]

ETHEL WIKOFF TEETERED AT the top of the ladder. James Nolen was doing a lousy job keeping it steady. The cool breeze blew through the Spanish moss hanging in the trees, and every noise in the dark cemetery behind the jail made him jump. James eyed the cast-iron balconies in the Moorish turret that rose above the four-story structure. What would they do if a guard saw them?

CHATHAM COUNTY JAIL, SAVANNAH, GA.

Chatham County Jail, Savannah, Georgia, circa 1930. *Courtesy of Savannah College of Art and Design.*

Ethel leaned as far as she could to hand Diggs a saw through his cell window. Usually, the attractive twenty-four-year-old partied with the most popular people in Memphis dressed in the most daring fashions, including skirts to her knees and bobbed hairstyles. Tonight, she was on a ladder outside her boyfriend's jail in Savannah. She had her reasons. The would-be gun moll wanted to make her mark in the underworld, and Diggs Nolen was her ticket.

Diggs got his fingers around the handle and pulled the saw in through his window. Ethel wobbled. The person described as one of the most beautiful women in Memphis unceremoniously tumbled off the ladder and landed in the weeds behind the jail. She was not quiet about it, either.

James heard men's voices and doors opening. He grabbed the injured Ethel and got her upright. He started to run but stopped when Ethel whimpered. James put an arm around her and helped her hobble across the dark cemetery. They ducked behind tombstones as the guards made it around the side of the jail and found the ladder.

Hours passed, and Diggs never appeared. The two gave up, slipped away and waited for further instructions from Holloway. Later, Ethel and James learned the guards had caught Diggs sawing through his bars and moved him to another cell.[35]

On November 25, Ethel sat with Diggs when he appeared in court before U.S. Commissioner W.R. Hewlett. Holloway hoped to sneak Diggs out of Georgia once he was released on bond, so he sent money with Ethel to cover the costs. Hewlett, however, set the bond at $6,000, far more than Holloway gave her. Without money for bail, Diggs remained in jail.[36]

Ethel pocketed the cash and took the train back to Memphis. She stayed with Ernest while she recuperated and corresponded with James through coded telegrams. She used aliases and indirect language to fool any police officer who might see their messages.

Meanwhile, Holloway came up with another plan to rescue Diggs. His gang would ambush the train carrying his cousin and free him from the U.S. marshals at gunpoint. It would take careful planning, so he first needed the train's itinerary. Ernest Nolen, who worked as a detective for the Memphis Police Department, wrote to the Savannah police chief, "Please wire me care of W.J. Hays Chief of Police, if Diggs Nolen, arrested by you, will come by Memphis on way to Omaha. He is my brother."[37]

When the telegram went unanswered, Holloway had Ethel contact James at the Geiger Hotel in Savannah on November 27 with a coded message. "Alice arrived OK. Get line on all trains and meet them," she wrote. "See Ticket agent and get direct route Mary goes over, get name of sleeper. Everything OK here… Answer this at once stating how everything is. Don't wait. Sarah." James got the train route and watched Diggs board the train. He responded on November 30, "Several officers left nine last night or six this morning via Atlanta heard would come through Memphis."[38]

The plan seemed too dangerous. James wondered if the better course of action would be to hire a lawyer for his son. He sent another coded telegram to Ethel. "You or Ernest come to Omaha at once," wrote James. "Bring all money you have and have balance sent on later. See C.W. Delamatre, attorney. When you arrive here I can send nor receive no messages. Geo."[39]

On December 5, James stepped aboard a train bound for Omaha. Ernest had assured his worried father that he only needed to provide Diggs's train schedule and "the boys here will do the rest."[40] He reread the telegram and wondered what the boys had in mind as he took his seat. He hardly noticed the sky had turned gray and storm clouds had moved in.

Chapter 4

THE LAD IN HANDCUFFS

Yet thou art doomed to mope in iron bars,
To bend thy proud young neck beneath a rod.
—Walter Malone, "The Lad in Handcuffs"[41]

Judge Walter Malone and his friend Daniel O'Donnell enjoyed their rides on the streetcar. They passed the time with small talk and discussions of current issues. They usually barely noticed the other passengers boarding or departing. A commotion at the door, however, caught their attention one day as a policeman dragged a teenager on board. Beat cops usually had to call for a police wagon to pick up prisoners, but rather than wait for a Black Maria, the officer instead was using a streetcar to take the teen to jail.

Malone and O'Donnell could not look away from the rough treatment of the manacled boy. How cruel was society to allow a child to be treated like a wild beast? The tragedy so moved Malone, an accomplished poet, that he wrote "The Lad in Handcuffs," one of his most memorable works.[42]

The boy, Kenny Bergin, worked part time as a messenger and part time as a petty thief. Like other children who committed crimes in the early twentieth century, Bergin would serve his jail sentences among adult offenders. As a teen, he became a hardened recidivist with a lengthy prison record. After a two-year sentence for burglary in the Louisiana State Penitentiary, he returned to Memphis and joined the Holloway Gang in 1912. The now twenty-one-year-old sought to prove himself to his new comrades by working his way from petty crimes to train robbery.[43]

Streetcars at Main Street Transfer Station, 1913. *Courtesy of Memphis Public Library and Information Center.*

Not every caper went so well, though. Bergin and nineteen-year-old Brantley "Country" Mitchell tried to rob a local businessman named Jules Stiffel in early December 1912. The two hoodlums pulled guns on Stiffel and ordered, "Hands up!" Stiffel surprised the two by drawing a handgun and firing on them. Bergin and Mitchell returned shots and escaped after slightly wounding Stiffel.[44]

In December 1912, Frank Holloway called on his gang to help him free his cousin. Bergin's pals meant everything to him, so it did not matter that he had never met Diggs Nolen. Diggs was important to them, so Diggs was important to him.

Holloway planned to ambush Diggs's train when it stopped in Memphis. Information from Diggs's father and train schedules supplied by former Frisco railroad agent John McCoy (a.k.a. Luther "Texas" Wallace) allowed Holloway to plan his attack. Holloway, McCoy, Mitchell, Jack Mundy and Bergen would overpower the marshals as they transferred Diggs to the connecting train. The bandits had guns, knives, skeleton keys, flashlights and other equipment. They also had wigs and police uniforms for disguises and current police reports supplied by Diggs's brother Ernest.[45]

Bergin listened as Holloway laid out a spectacular rescue with blazing guns and an escape on horseback. After mulling it over for a few days, however, the seasoned railway bandit toned down his plan. Holloway decided an armed rescue in the crowded train station would be too dangerous, so he opted instead to ambush the train before it arrived.

Bergin was eager for another train caper. In February 1912, he helped the gang rob a train bound for Oklahoma City near Hulburt, Arkansas. Three of the gang boarded as passengers in Memphis. Once the train crossed the bridge into Arkansas, they crawled across the roof of their passenger car to get to the engine. They held the engineer and firemen at gunpoint and ordered them to stop the train. Three more masked gunmen appeared from the woods and joined them.[46]

Brantley "Country" Mitchell, Memphis Police Department mug shot, circa 1912. *Courtesy of Memphis Public Library and Information Center.*

The gunmen ordered the crew to disconnect the mail cars and leave, so they had to hurry before the engineer reached the next stop and reported the robbery to the sheriff. They ransacked the mail for money and valuables and used nitroglycerin to blow open the safes.

They knew how to stop a train, but they were not experts with explosives. The blast blew the cars to pieces and sent the safes hurtling through the air. The safes smashed open on impact and scattered money throughout the flaming debris. The thieves saved $60,000 from burning and escaped on horseback before the posse arrived.[47]

Holloway considered the robbery a success and hoped to have the same luck liberating Diggs. On Monday, December 9, 1912, the gang boarded the train they thought carried Diggs when it stopped at a water station outside Memphis. The bandits held the crew and passengers at gunpoint until they realized it was the wrong train. Holloway had to decide what to do. He only had a small window of opportunity to rescue his cousin from the next train, because the passengers on this train would surely notify the police when they arrived at the station. Holloway decided to take a chance. He let the train leave and waited for the next one.[48]

The next train stopped at the water station. The bandits once again drew their weapons and tried to board. However, this time, they found a contingent of deputy marshals waiting for them. A gunfight broke out, and the bandits had to retreat empty-handed. They escaped under a hail of gunfire and fled to their safe house on the outskirts of the city.[49]

BERGIN KEPT WATCH FOR the posse from the garret window in his upstairs bedroom. Hours passed, but no one came. Tired of staring out the window, he got into a bed where he could still see the street. Eventually, the cold, quiet night lulled him to sleep.

Earlier that day, chief of detectives James Roper received a tip that the Holloway Gang was hiding at 1157 Wilson Street near the southern city limit. Roper called in seven of his detectives. The bandits had no fear of shooting it out with police, so Roper told his team to sneak up on the bandits in the early morning hours to catch them off guard.

Bergin slept as Detectives Powell Covey, John Klinck, Will Smiddy, John Foppiano, Frank Turner, Oliver Hazard Perry and Al Hurst gathered outside. The dead grass crunched under their shoes, and they could see their breath in the moonlight. Cold fingers held shotguns and pistols as they split up and circled the house.

A soft knock on the front door roused Mrs. McCoy. Cold and sleepy, she peeked through the curtains and thought she saw Country Mitchell. She opened the door, ready to scold the young man. She gasped. It was not Mitchell waiting for her but instead several armed strangers.

Memphis police detective Will Smiddy. *Courtesy of Memphis Public Library and Information Center.*

Mrs. McCoy stumbled backward, away from the reaching hands. She wanted to call out, but Smiddy had his hand over her mouth. She kicked and writhed under his grip, knocking over furniture. Smiddy pinned her down as the other detectives poured through the door and snatched the sleeping Mitchell and McCoy.

Holloway's dog barked at the commotion. The bandit's eyes snapped open, and he threw off his blanket. He rolled off the bed onto the floor and fumbled for his pistol. The door flew open, and an angry voice shouted at him. His eyes adjusted to the light and focused on the shotgun leveled at his face. The bandit growled and cursed. The coppers had the jump on him. Instead of reaching for his pistol, he reached for the sky.[50]

Upstairs, Bergin grabbed his pair of revolvers, but he knew he did not have a chance against all those armed men. A lone detective, John Foppiano, stood watch in the yard below. He liked his odds against this fellow better. Bergin opened the garret window and fired a shot that sent the detective scrambling for cover.

Bergin crawled out the window and fired again at Foppiano. The bandit's bare feet nearly froze on the shingles of the slanted roof. The detective returned fire as Bergin hid behind a chimney. The shivering young man struggled to find a secure foothold. Bergin took aim again but slipped and tumbled off the roof before he could get another shot off. He bounced off a drainpipe and landed in the backyard.

Memphis police detective John Foppiano. *Courtesy of Memphis Public Library and Information Center.*

Bergin fired again when Foppiano circled the house. The detective ducked, and Bergin bolted. Bergin jumped a fence and made a run for it. Foppiano followed, but Bergin ran down the nearby railroad tracks and disappeared in the dark. Steam rose off Foppiano as he slowed to a walk. He caught his ragged breath and turned back to the house. He had no reason to chase Bergin. He knew a half-dressed man could not go far in freezing weather.[51]

Bergin ran for about half a mile along the railroad tracks until he got to South Parkway East, a major thoroughfare. He walked five blocks to a grocery store at the corner of College Street. The pajama-clad Bergin told the grocer an angry husband had caught him with his wife. He claimed he escaped by jumping through a window as the husband shot at him. Either out of pity or a sense of humor, the grocer handed Bergin some pants, shoes and a coat. Bergin promised to return them and left one of his pistols as collateral.[52]

Meanwhile, Smiddy stood watch as the other detectives searched Holloway's safe house. The police heard rumors the gang had a stash of money and nitroglycerin. Not much turned up, but they found gold watches and valuables taken in previous robberies.

As they searched, a man in an overcoat came up the street toward the house. As he came closer, Smiddy recognized him as Bergin. The detective ordered the young man to surrender, but Bergin only locked eyes with Smiddy. Bergin reached into his borrowed coat as Smiddy dropped his hand to his sidearm. The two pulled their pistols and opened fire at one another.

The gunfire sent the detectives scrambling outside to help Smiddy. Once the other detectives opened fire, Bergin had too many targets and not enough cover. He turned to dash for a better position when something struck him in the back. A burning sensation spread below his left shoulder, and a heaviness settled in his chest. His body went numb, and he dropped to the frozen pavement, where he took his last breath.[53]

"We had men watching Atlanta and Birmingham," grumbled Holloway, "and we were in Memphis, but the dicks [detectives] gave us the slip." The marshals had intercepted Ethel Wikoff's telegrams and secretly transferred Diggs to a different train when they reached Macon, Georgia.[54] Diggs's train bypassed Memphis on his way to Omaha, while at the same time, another group of marshals stayed on the original train to catch the would-be rescuers.[55]

Holloway, angry about being so easily duped, accused Ethel of informing the police. In the parlance of the time, he said he "doped out" that she "peached" and kept the money intended for Diggs's bond for herself. Detective Oliver Perry, however, dismissed the idea that Ethel betrayed the gang. "Holloway does not know where I got the tip [about the gang's location], and he is not likely to find out," said Perry.[56]

Holloway, always eager to talk, made a long, exaggerated confession. He treated his time in the interrogation room as a soliloquy and the police as his audience. He shared the details of his aborted rescue and claimed to have money and explosives hidden at the safe house.[57]

From a separate cell, Country Mitchell laughed at detectives when they said they had Holloway in custody. They wanted to know about the nitroglycerin Holloway claimed he buried in metal containers. "You are all a big bunch of dubs," yelled Mitchell from behind bars. "You haven't got Frank Holloway locked up at all. You won't get him. He is too smart for you!"[58]

Bergin's unclaimed body lay at Thompson Brothers' Mortuary. The detectives could only speculate as to why Bergin returned to the house after making his escape. They asked Holloway. The gang leader would only say that he would explain everything later, but how could he? How could he make them understand the outlaw code of loyalty?

Chapter 5
ERNEST NOLEN

I was sorry as I could be for doing what I did…
but you know blood runs thicker than water.
—*Ernest L. Nolen*[59]

Detective Ernest Nolen's distinguished military record from his service during the Spanish-American War had helped win him a position with the police department. He served in Cuba in the Fifth U.S. Volunteers, took part in the Battle of San Juan and later served in the Twenty-Ninth U.S. Volunteers in the Philippines. In 1909, Ernest helped Mississippi veterans secure drawings for land allotments in the Dakotas.[60]

By all accounts, Ernest Nolen performed his duties as a detective admirably. He had a promising career, but his loyalty to his brother and cousins proved stronger than his sense of duty. Fire and police commissioner R.A. Utley said Ernest had "borne the very best sort of reputation heretofore, but the presence of the men [Holloway's gang] in the city for about a month, and the failure of the detective to report that fact to the chief, was something that the department could not overlook."[61]

On December 9, 1912, Mayor Edward Hull Crump met with Utley and police chief William J. Hayes about Ernest's role in Frank Holloway's botched rescue of Diggs Nolen. They heard from witnesses who saw him talking to Holloway on the street before the rescue attempt and fellow officers who rode with Ernest on the trolley when he visited the gang's safe house. However, the most substantial evidence came from John McCoy's wife, who detailed Ernest's involvement in the plot.[62]

Left: Memphis police detective Ernest Nolen, brother of Diggs Nolen. *Courtesy of Memphis Public Library and Information Center.*

Right: Mayor Edward Hull Crump. *Courtesy of Memphis Public Library and Information Center.*

"If Mayor Crump will come to me, and listen to what I have to say, I can explain away everything that would tend to reflect on Ernest Nolen," said Holloway from his cell. Holloway vehemently denied Ernest knew of the plot or the gang's presence in Memphis. "I would just as soon let [Memphis Police] Chief Roper know I was here as Ernest," vowed Holloway. Utley and Hayes did not take Holloway's claims any more seriously than his boasts about his criminal record. They followed Crump's orders and fired Ernest.[63]

Ernest called the charges a political "frame-up" and proclaimed his innocence while all along secretly planning another jailbreak for his brother. Ernest recruited John M. Jones, his partner in the barbershop he ran on the side and friend since their service during the Spanish-American War. They bought supplies, including rope and hacksaws, and left for Omaha.[64]

Police suspected Ernest would try again to free his brother, so they coordinated with the U.S. Department of Justice and the Omaha Police Department to monitor his movements. A government agent followed Ernest and Jones on the train to Omaha. He watched as Ernest rented a room in a boardinghouse under the alias Robert E. Lee and met with another cousin, Ralph Burns (a.k.a. Tobie Dunn) to prepare for the jailbreak.[65]

Diggs Nolen appeared before Judge William Munger on December 21, 1912, and pleaded not guilty to fraud charges. Munger bound him over to the January term, when he would go on trial. Diggs fumed over his pending sentence and agonized over the death of Kenny Bergin. Diggs's prospects seemed bleak until he received a message that his brother planned to free him.[66]

Ernest enlisted the help of jail trustee Alfred Gallahue to lower nine steel saws on a string from the jail's roof to Diggs's window during the night. He also gave Diggs a code to signal his brother, who waited in the shadows across the street. Ernest, Jones and Dunn would lift their hats to signal that Gallahue had lowered the last package. Diggs would then light two matches in sequence to indicate he received the message.[67]

Secrets, however, are hard to keep in jail. Harry Seaman, another prisoner, overheard Gallahue and Diggs and notified a jailer of the escape plans. On January 7, 1913, Seaman told Sheriff Felix McShane that Gallahue delivered the package to Diggs. The sheriff searched the cell, found the tools and saw cuts in the bars. The jailers moved Diggs to solitary confinement and arrested Burns when he tried to visit Diggs. Police tried to capture Ernest and Jones, but the two escaped to Memphis to gather money and their belongings before fleeing west.[68]

Diggs appeared in court the next day. Law enforcement officers from eight states sat in the courtroom ready with requisition papers to arrest Diggs should the Omaha jury find him not guilty. Diggs and the Holloway Gang had, in the previous year, swindled people in Tennessee, New Mexico, Colorado, Missouri, Texas, Nebraska, Arkansas and Illinois. The jury, surprised he would not take the stand in his defense, found Diggs guilty of using the mail to defraud and using fictitious matter to defraud. Officers, fearing Diggs would attempt another escape, rushed him to Kansas and had him securely behind bars within twenty-four hours.[69]

Ernest and Jones returned to Memphis to find police waiting for them. Once in custody, Ernest told Jones to stay quiet. Jones, however, confessed and implicated Ernest and Ethel not only in the plot to free Diggs from the Omaha jail but also the attempted jailbreak in Savannah. Ernest told his wife from his cell, "Jones, my best friend, has gone bad on me. Jones has told everything on me. I will fix him for telling."[70]

The U.S. Marshals Service assigned six officers armed with Winchester rifles to ward off any rescue attempt. Marshal J.S. Johnson told reporters, "Not even [Ernest] Nolen's wife will know when he leaves or what route my deputies take to Omaha. I have always liked Nolen personally, and when he was a city detective, he always gave my office considerable assistance. But he seems to have become mixed up in bad company, and we will take no chances when we leave Memphis with him."[71]

Friends and relatives had already begun to lobby for an early release when Ernest arrived at Leavenworth Federal Prison in April 1913. Senator James K. Vardaman of Mississippi had served in the military with Ernest and considered him a friend; he gladly delivered a petition from Ernest's parents and wife to President Woodrow Wilson. Wilson granted the pardon in October 1913, and the former city detective came back to Memphis and resumed working as a barber.[72]

Jones's testimony implicated Ethel Wikoff as well. U.S. marshals arrested her in Muskogee, Oklahoma, where she worked as a clerk in a cigar store. Ethel lied about her name and denied any knowledge of the Nolens. The marshals, however, brought Ernest and Gallahue along to confirm her identity. A special federal grand jury indicted her on charges of conspiracy to liberate a federal prisoner and extradited her to Omaha.[73]

Two spectacular attempts to free Diggs Nolen had failed miserably. Diggs was no closer to freedom, and his would-be liberators now faced prison terms as well. Diggs arrived at Leavenworth Prison on January 12, 1913. He was fingerprinted, photographed and examined by the prison doctor. His release would have been September 18, 1916, at the earliest, had he served his time without incident. Diggs, however, never went for long without causing an incident.

Chapter 6
THOMAS MORGAN

Don't do anything to betray the confidence the officers have in you.
—Ella Nolen to Diggs Nolen

Thomas Morgan believed in the possibility of redemption. The square-shouldered, gray-eyed, fifty-one-year-old warden of Leavenworth Federal Prison based his approach to his job on this belief. For Morgan, a prison sentence served as more than punishment; it was a chance for prisoners to rehabilitate, learn a new skill and become productive members of society. A person, given a chance, could make amends for past mistakes.

Morgan's interest in prisons led him to serve as the Kansas State Board of Penal Institutions president. Before that, he taught school and ran the Ottawa newspaper the *Republican*, which he renamed the *Daily Republic*. He turned down the Kansas governor's offer to make him warden of the state prison in January 1913 but changed his mind when President Woodrow Wilson's attorney general, James Clark McReynolds, offered him the position of warden to the federal prison at Leavenworth in June 1913.[74]

Morgan devised a plan to modernize Leavenworth after visiting the new federal prison at Atlanta. He requested appropriations for construction projects, improved the food and held sporting events for the inmates. He also allowed prisoners to earn money to help them get a fresh start.[75]

Morgan's most important program provided legal assistance to prisoners trying to initiate habeas corpus cases. Prisoners could now submit copies of their indictments and commitment papers to the district attorney and

Leavenworth Prison, 1910. *Courtesy of Library of Congress.*

request the help of an attorney in preparing a petition. Before, the court frequently threw out petitions because of technical errors on the part of the prisoners. Prisoners now had as much chance of success as those who had the twenty-five or thirty dollars to hire a lawyer.[76]

Convicted safecracker Richard "Tricksey" Osbourne learned that just because Morgan wanted to run a progressive prison, that didn't mean he was a pushover. Osbourne and counterfeiter Walter Layman escaped just as Robert Wilson McClaughry turned the prison over to the new warden. Osbourne and Layman arranged clothes to look like they were sleeping in their bunks, sawed through the bars in the window, climbed a wall and jumped into a waiting getaway car. News broke about the escape on June 30, 1913, the same day Morgan published his farewell in the *Daily Republic*.[77]

After his capture in Seattle, Osbourne wanted to make a grand entrance back into the prison population. Osbourne smugly told Morgan that he timed his escape to save the new warden from embarrassment and for that, Morgan owed Osbourne a favor. He promised to behave for six months if Morgan would go easy on him. Osbourne wanted to brag to the other inmates that he had outsmarted the rookie warden, but his ploy backfired. Instead of allowing Osbourne the fanfare he craved, Morgan sent Osbourne to isolation and had him break rocks for a month. By the time Osbourne returned to the general population, the inmates had forgotten about his escapade.[78]

Diggs Nolen, on other hand, seemed to Morgan like a man ready to rehabilitate. Diggs, now Inmate 8453, arrived at Leavenworth Prison on January 12, 1913, with his sentence scheduled to end on September 18, 1916. The twenty-five-year-old remained in good health for the most part, despite some dental work, occasional bouts of grippe, malaria and complications from gonorrhea. The college-educated Diggs had a profession and family and friends who said he could turn his life around. All believed that Diggs was a good person who had just fallen in with bad company.[79]

Diggs, however, struggled to keep up the image created for him. Diggs lost five days of good time when he refused to help clean the dispensary in February 1913. Indignant at receiving what he thought was a Black man's work, he told the guard, "I see where we are not going to get along. I am not a porter." The guards reprimanded Diggs for talking when he was supposed to be quiet, refusing to work, taking another prisoner's chair and wasting food. Even after Morgan's arrival, Diggs got into a fight with another prisoner and refused to work.[80]

Diggs's supporters appealed to Morgan to make him a trusty. Senator Luke Lea of Tennessee, newspaper editor C.P.J. Mooney and Memphis

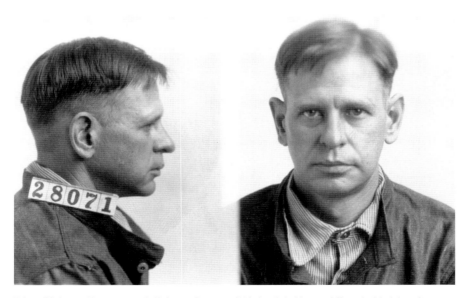

Diggs Nolen at Leavenworth Prison. *Courtesy of National Archives and Records Administration.*

Leavenworth Prison, prisoners marching to dinner, 1910. *Courtesy of Library of Congress.*

justice of the peace W.L. Kearney vouched for Diggs. Morgan took the recommendations to heart and made Diggs a trusty on January 13, 1914. The position allowed Diggs better housing, easier work and less supervision. It also helped build the case that Diggs had been rehabilitated.[81]

Morgan replied to Senator Lea, "[Diggs] so far has lived up to the obligations of his position." He allowed Diggs to correspond with family and friends, who tried to help him get a presidential pardon, including Senator James Vardaman of Mississippi and Senator Thomas Upton Sisson of Mississippi. Even Mayor Edward Hull Crump of Memphis voiced his support for Diggs's early release.[82]

Things were looking up for Diggs. He had a light workload, he took a correspondence course and Morgan allowed him to have subscriptions to magazines like the *Saturday Evening Post*. Morgan offered Diggs better accommodations, but he turned them down to share a cell with his brother Ernest.[83]

Even so, not everyone trusted Diggs. U.S. Attorney F.S. Howell warned Morgan's predecessor, R.W. McClaughry, that he should keep Diggs under careful watch. Howell, who prosecuted Diggs, advised the warden to keep James Nolen from communicating with his son because he might initiate another escape. Nevertheless, Morgan did not take the warnings seriously. After all, why would a prisoner poised to receive a pardon want to escape?[84]

DIGGS NOLEN OPENED THE letter from his mother hoping it would bring good news. She had recently moved from Mississippi to Loveland, Colorado, believing the change in climate might help her tuberculosis. The disease affects the lungs, but it can spread to other organs, including the gastrointestinal and genitourinary tracts, bones, joints, nervous system, lymph nodes and skin. Tuberculosis, commonly called consumption, and pneumonia were the two leading causes of death in the early 1900s. Tuberculosis killed slowly, and patients might be coughing up infected sputum for years as the disease gradually destroyed their lungs and wasted their bodies.[85]

Ella Nolen led friends and relatives in a letter-writing campaign for her son's release. She understood that winning a pardon would take time and patience, even with the help of a sympathetic warden. Ella also knew her son's mercurial nature better than most. She warned Diggs, "Don't do anything to betray the confidence the officers have in you." She worried that she might not live to see her son's release. She also worried that her son might do something impulsive and ruin his chances for a pardon.[86]

Diggs grew increasingly anxious over his mother's declining health. He wrote to Senator Lea asking him to persuade President Wilson to issue a pardon "before it is too late." Friendly lawmakers had promised to talk to the

Leavenworth Prison Dormitory, 1910. *Courtesy of Library of Congress.*

president for weeks. Didn't they understand that his mother was sick? Time was running out, and all he could do was write more letters. Or was it?[87]

On July 22, after mailing letters to Williams and Lea, Diggs gave in to his impulses and escaped during the night. The following morning, Thomas Morgan sat down at his desk to write a letter to the U.S. attorney general. Morgan was typically an optimistic person, but on this day, he felt discouraged. Reporting an escape was never easy, but owning up to being duped was humiliating. As Morgan wrote, he had to admit that rehabilitation could be an elusive prize.

Chapter 7
ESCAPE FROM LEAVENWORTH

The only surprise to me was that he did not escape a long time ago.
—U.S. district attorney F.S. Howell[88]

Ernest Nolen, after hearing about the nationwide manhunt for his brother, wrote to Warden Morgan to assure him that he and his mother had not seen his brother. Ernest, who stayed with his mother in Loveland, wrote that she did not have long to live and her heart was broken by Diggs's escape. He assured the warden, "I have tried to be a good Christian ever since I got in trouble two years ago and I shall never do wrong again." When asked about the whereabouts of his fugitive brother, Ernest told reporters that Diggs was leading a "straight-forward life" in Canada.[89]

Department of Justice special agent William McElveen wrote to Morgan, "The circumstances look suspicious." He, like Morgan, had received a letter from Ernest. McElveen doubted Ernest's promises that he and his family had not harbored Diggs. He told Morgan he thought it was suspicious that Ernest moved to Loveland just before Diggs's escape. McElveen assigned agents to keep an eye on the Nolens, but by then, Diggs had already left his parent's home.[90]

After leaving Loveland, Diggs spent most of his time on the run in Texas and Louisiana, possibly in the company of his new girlfriend, Helen Rosser. Morgan contacted the Pinkerton Detective Agency and chiefs of police and sheriffs from Tennessee to Arizona. He sent twenty-two thousand flyers out with Diggs's Bertillon description and asked the post office to monitor the mail of Ernest, Ella and Ethel. He also wrote to everyone who sent a letter recommending Diggs as a trusty to let each one know about his escape. Weeks went by without a lead.[91]

Police almost captured Diggs on September 30, 1914. An officer arrested Diggs as he snuck out the second-story window of the Majestic Hotel in Fort Worth. Diggs used an alias and claimed to be an out-of-work field hand. He offered to pawn his suit to pay the hotel bill, but the arresting officer refused. Instead, Diggs left the suitcase with the hotel manager and said he would return with the money owed. Another young man returned, paid the outstanding bill and collected the suitcase. The hotel manager and the officer thought the matter closed until later, when the officer noticed a wanted poster at the police station. The patrolman matched Diggs to a Bertillon record and realized his mistake. By then, it was too late. Diggs got away.[92]

The most sensational sighting of Diggs came on the morning of January 27, 1915, when three armed and masked men burst into the Houston Guaranty Bank in Houston, Texas, and demanded money. One man forced the bank staff into a vault while the others filled sacks with money. As the three fled on foot to their hideout, one of the money bags ripped open. A trail of silver dollars led police to the gang's hideout in the rear of a small store, where after a brief gunfight, the three wounded bandits surrendered. Bank tellers identified the robbers as Johnnie Bowman, Hart Austin and Diggs Nolen. Excitement about Diggs's arrest spread quickly until police realized the man they thought was Diggs was really Diggs's cousin Floyd Nolen.[93]

DIGGS NOLEN SCOOPED THE nickels into his pocket. A cool, moist breeze blew in from the Gulf of Mexico, and the noise of the harbor filled the air. He could see ships at the New Orleans dock from the windows as he emptied the coin box of the payphone in the train station at the foot of Canal Street. Diggs had been robbing telephone boxes with five other men since he arrived in New Orleans in late 1914. The gang netted around $200 a week with keys supplied by another Memphian simply known as King.[94]

An African American porter saw Diggs fumbling with the change and chased him across the station. They weaved between the passengers in the crowded general waiting room. Before Diggs could get to the exit, the porter caught up with him and pulled a pistol. Diggs surrendered and waited for the police to arrive. Diggs gave his name as George Williams, but the officers recognized him from his wanted posters.[95]

Canal Street, New Orleans, Louisiana, 1910. *Courtesy of Library of Congress.*

News of the arrest spread quickly. Ella Diggs begged Thomas Morgan for leniency and promised her son would behave like a good Christian. The warden assured her that he harbored no grudge and would treat her son fairly. He allowed Diggs to see friends and relatives, take another correspondence course and subscribe to magazines and newspapers. Morgan gave Diggs's parents updates and encouragement after they moved to Douglas, Arizona, on the U.S.-Mexico border.[96]

Diggs, however, had more interest in keeping in touch with Helen Rosser. The young woman pleaded with Morgan to continue communicating with Diggs, but Morgan thought romantic correspondence between a married man and an unmarried woman inappropriate. Morgan relented only after Diggs admitted that he was never married to Ethel Wikoff.[97]

In March 1917, Helen wrote from Texarkana: "You are positively a darling. Your advice is so refreshing. It relieves the horrible monotony. No doubt I am everything you say. You have interested me greatly. I never suspected you of being such a devil. Do it again. I really like it even after today's occurrence. I still love you and will send you the Nabiscos surely. You

Train Terminal, New Orleans, Louisiana, 1910. *Courtesy of Library of Congress.*

will write to acknowledge this and thank me for the cake. Do you really think I am a very bad guy?"[98]

Diggs telegrammed Helen telling her to come visit him. On May 17, 1917, Helen replied, "On my return from Shreveport found your wife of yesterday [Ethel]. Therefore, the delay. I will try very hard to come next week. I can't promise positively to come until after the first of June. Is your need urgent? Write particulars. So glad that you wrote me. Love, Helen."[99]

Meanwhile, momentum picked up in the campaign for Diggs's early release. In January 1916, Morgan informed Senator Lea that Diggs's case was "worthy of executive clemency." In February 1917, the U.S. attorney general shortened Diggs's sentence by restoring 240 days of time lost due to the escape. On December 9, 1917, after Senators Vardaman, Williams and Sisson assured President Wilson that Diggs ran away only to see his dying mother, Wilson issued a full pardon.[100]

Diggs left Leavenworth and briefly sold insurance in Little Rock, Arkansas. He became restless, borrowed twenty-five dollars from billiard hall owner and boxing promoter Bob O'Rourke and left for Oklahoma. Diggs tried to enlist for military service to fight in Europe, but the draft board would not take him because of his prison record and lack of permanent residence. He eventually took his mother's advice, returned to Memphis and opened his first pharmacy.[101]

Morgan's political enemies accused him of embezzling money from the fund he created to help recently released prisoners. The judge dismissed the charges, but the investigation left Morgan disgusted with the toxic environment of state politics. He kept contact with the Nolens after he resigned and returned home to Ottawa, Kansas. Morgan took some comfort in his success with Diggs, but he knew lasting rehabilitation depended on the young man staying free of bad influences.

Chapter 8

NARCOTICS

We don't know yet what we're charged with, and we don't give a whoop!
—Pearl Griffin Hunt

Diggs Nolen's promises to become a law-abiding Christian lasted about as long as it took to buy his first pharmacy. On the surface, his store at South Main and Talbot seemed like a respectable, albeit mundane, business. He filled prescriptions and sold sodas and cigars as any other pharmacist. Beneath the surface, however, the quaint corner drugstore served as a cover for a criminal operation that won Diggs the title "King of the Memphis Underworld."

Diggs was tapping into a black market inadvertently created by the U.S. government. The Harrison Anti-Narcotic Act went into effect on March 1, 1915, and made the sale of narcotics illegal without a prescription. The federal government required doctors and pharmacists to register, record their drug transactions and, most importantly, apply for a special revenue stamp. The new federal law superseded the Tennessee law passed a year earlier requiring a prescription from a doctor with a special permit to purchase narcotics. Advocates of the new law naively believed it would make addiction a thing of the past; instead, it pushed the narcotics market underground.[102]

The Shanghai Opium Convention in 1909 and the First International Opium Convention in 1911 provided the impetus for the law. After attending the conventions, Ohio doctor Hamilton Wright played on fears of addiction by exaggerating statistics. He convinced Representative Francis

Burton Harrison to support anti-narcotics legislation in the U.S. House of Representatives. The U.S. Congress passed the bill, and President Woodrow Wilson signed it into law in 1914.

According to the act, a doctor could prescribe and distribute narcotics "in the course of his professional practice" and in "good faith." While meant to prohibit the distribution of drugs to recreational users, the law lacked clarity in defining the scope of a doctor's "professional practice." Lawyers argued over whether it was part of a doctor's practice to give drugs to an addict to ease withdrawal symptoms. Meanwhile, those who had developed opioid addictions following injuries, surgeries or childbirth suffered miserably.[103]

Pharmacists and doctors scrambled to get permits to avoid fines of up to $2,000 and possible jail sentences of up to five years. Over three thousand Tennessee pharmacists registered to dispense narcotics within the first week of the law's enactment, but not everyone made the deadline. In Memphis, U.S. marshals arrested medical professionals for noncompliance, while police launched raids on opium dens and street dealers.[104]

The restrictions caused a spike in national crime rates. Addicts turned to street dealers who charged exorbitant prices for drugs, and in turn, addicts resorted to crime to raise money to pay them. In Memphis, police periodically rounded up suspected drug users to curb robberies. In December 1919, police arrested a dozen addicted "burglars and sneak thieves" in one night and a dozen more before noon the next day.[105]

The Harrison Anti-Narcotic Act only exacerbated the narcotics problem for police in Memphis. After cocaine, arrived in the 1890s, three out of four people arrested were high on the drug. Street dealers, pharmacies and grocery stores sold cocaine in five- and ten-cent boxes. Police told Mayor J.J. Williams that cocaine addiction had reached such an alarming extent that police could not "cope with its ravages." Williams pushed for an ordinance limiting sales to pharmacies, but it did little good. The situation only worsened as morphine, which sold on the street for thirty-five dollars an ounce, eclipsed cocaine as the drug of choice. Arrest records alone indicated that the city had over five hundred addicts by 1922. Police picked them up for possession or panhandling, but Shelby County Workhouse officials refused to hold addicts because of the limited facilities.[106]

Dr. Lucius P. Brown, chief of the Tennessee Department of Food and Drugs, hoped to break the cycle of addiction and crime by simply giving drugs to registered addicts. By 1915, the state had issued 2,401 permits for morphine, 120 for gum opium, 191 for opium extracts and 31 for heroin. The state registered 1,609 White females, 161 African American females,

539 White males and 44 African American males. Dr. Brown, however, suspected the rolls contained no more than a quarter of the state's addicts.[107]

In March 1915, Memphis police set up a temporary hospital for addicts in the Tri-State Fairgrounds amusement park. Hundreds flocked to the so-called dope lines to receive their allotments of morphine from the police department's surgeon. Police encouraged morphine addicts to come to the facility but sent cocaine addicts to the Shelby County Workhouse, where doctors believed they could recover from their addictions without help.[108]

Addicts, not satisfied with their tiny rations, continued to buy drugs off the black market. In 1918, Newark, New Jersey neurologist Dr. Charles A. Rosewater made a study of the rising use of morphine and cocaine in cities around the country.[109] In Memphis, Rosewater found that criminals from around the country were going to the city because of the ease of acquiring narcotics. He estimated that addicts purchased between fifteen and twenty-two thousand doses of morphine in Memphis every year in addition to vast amounts of cocaine, opium, heroin and caffeinated soft drinks. By 1918, Memphis had the most formidable gang of "bootleggers in drugs" in the United States next to New York City and San Francisco. Rosewater called the city the center of narcotic traffic in America.[110]

The Tri-State Fairgrounds in Memphis. *Courtesy of Memphis Public Library and Information Center.*

Dr. J.L. Andrews of the Memphis Board of Health oversaw the filling of police surgeon Dr. J.L. Drake's prescriptions for addicts. Andrews could not keep up with so many prescriptions, so in October 1919, police medical personnel began dispensing drugs again, this time directly from their headquarters. Addicts paid five cents per grain of morphine, far less than the twenty-five cents street dealers charged. The chemist mixed the drug with a drinkable liquid solution to avoid hypodermic needles.[111]

Andrews still could not supply every addict, so he turned to local pharmacists to help fill prescriptions. Police, however, had shut down many pharmacists for noncompliance with the state regulations and licensing. The crackdown left Diggs Nolen as one of the few pharmacists willing or able to help. Diggs eagerly filled the void and soon had a near monopoly on filling narcotic prescriptions.

Those without prescriptions begged for a dollar's worth of drugs, a capsule or just a tablet to ease their withdrawals. Diggs's willingness to bend the rules soon won him a loyal following of addicts. They eagerly sought out Diggs for his drugs, and he accepted their stolen goods as payment, which, in turn, he sold to criminals in New York City. The only problem Diggs faced was how to get around the ever-tightening regulations. Diggs could make much more money if he could get drugs without creating a paper trail.[112]

Diggs found his solution in a pair of sisters looking to make easy money. Twenty-year-old Jessie Griffin Cannoy and her eighteen-year-old sister Pearl Griffin Hunt had been rebellious girls and friends of many well-known and flamboyant recidivists, commonly called police characters. Jessie ran away from her home in Tulsa when she was sixteen and married against her father's wishes. At seventeen, Pearl married a hoodlum named Adolph Hunt shortly before his deployment overseas to fight in France with Jessie's new husband. Not satisfied to live on the thirty-dollar monthly allotment from the government for their husbands' service in the army, the sisters approached Diggs, a man well known in the underworld, about selling drugs.[113]

In November 1918, Diggs sent Jessie, Pearl and his cousin Floyd Nolen to Little Rock, Arkansas, with a phony permit. Local wholesale drug houses had stopped selling large quantities of narcotics, making Little Rock the closest source for narcotics in bulk. Floyd went along with the plan to pay back a loan, and the sisters just loved the idea of being outlaws. Diggs sent these two country girls, barely out of their teens, and his bank-robbing cousin, whom police captured after following a trail of coins, with $1,250 and falsified documents to score the modern equivalent of half a million dollars' worth of narcotics. What could go wrong?[114]

JESSIE AND PEARL BUNDLED up and headed for the station to meet Floyd Nolen. The sun had been up for only a little more than an hour when their train left Memphis. The train for Little Rock rattled over the Harahan Bridge, crossed the Mississippi River and headed for the flat expanse of eastern Arkansas.[115]

A few hours later, Floyd, Jessie and Pearl saw the tiled roof and flagpole on the Missouri Pacific Train Station tower across the Arkansas River. They stepped off the train, crossed the platform and made their way to Markham Street. They walked about a mile in the afternoon sun to Joe and Sam Storthz's jewelry and pawnshop at the corner of Main Street.

Salesman Charlie Siegel looked up when the fellow with the two young women came through the door. The customers scanned the shelves and asked about purchasing a couple of large trunks. Siegel gave them a price, and they asked if he could put Yale locks on them. He told them he could, but he could not finish that day. The trio planned to leave the following morning, so they settled on a couple of old suitcases instead.[116]

Floyd paid Siegel and stepped away from the counter. In hushed tones, he went over the last-minute details of the plan to buy the drugs with the sisters. Floyd wanted to split up in case anything went wrong, so he told them to meet

Union Station in Memphis. *Courtesy of Memphis Public Library and Information Center.*

him at a rendezvous point after the purchase. The plan required a degree of subtlety that Pearl did not have, so Jessie told her to wait in the pawnshop.[117]

Jessie walked a few doors down to the John B. Bond Wholesale Drug Company and introduced herself to the clerk, G.S. Paschal, as the wife of Memphis druggist J.N. Thompson. The clerk was polite but suspicious.

Pascal asked how he could help.

"I want morphine."

"How much?" asked Paschal.

"All you've got."

Paschal hesitated at the unusual request but filled the order when Jessie presented the forged permit. As she pulled out cash to pay, Jessie told T.E. Lucas, head of the shipping department, to put the drugs in the two old suitcases. It was a tremendous score for the newbie drug trafficker. Once Lucas finished packing, Jessie had 540 vials of morphine and an additional 80 vials of cocaine.[118]

As Lucas packed the suitcases, Paschal slipped back into the office. Something was not right. The young woman's demeanor made him uneasy, so he made some telephone calls to check her story. Lucas finished, and Jessie telephoned for a taxi from the counter. Jessie hobbled out the door with a heavy suitcase in each hand to wait for her ride. All she had to do was get her sister and get in the cab and she was home free. She had taken a few steps toward the pawnshop when she saw internal revenue agents J.B. Greeson and J.E. Greene waiting to arrest her. Paschal had figured out Jessie's ploy and tipped off the agents.[119]

The arrest of Jessie and Pearl brought up questions about the druggist's practices. John B. Bond defended his company's policies: "There are no restrictions on a wholesale druggist in the sale of morphine and other drugs. It is not our business to ascertain what the purchaser is to do with the purchase, as long as the purchaser has the proper government [forms], properly filled out, we may sell any amount of drugs to him he desires." Bond explained, "We could have had no way of knowing last Tuesday that the sale was not for another jobber."[120]

At the courthouse, Jessie shrugged off the high bond. "All right, pardner," she acquiesced in her best cowboy drawl as she followed the deputy to jail. Agent Greeson had recommended a high bond because he expected the sisters' confederates to put up the money and then help them escape. Diggs Nolen did not want to implicate himself by paying the bond, so he had Jim Whitten, one of his pharmacy employees, wire $400 to boxing promoter Bob O'Rourke at his pool hall in Little Rock to pay for the sisters' lawyer.[121]

After five weeks in jail, Jessie and Pearl still refused to cooperate with prosecutors. They had fun pointing out friends' pictures in the station's "rogues' gallery" while waiting to be photographed and have Bertillon measurements taken. Pearl told a reporter, "We don't know yet what we're charged with, and we don't give a whoop!" She was glad to be out of the cold January weather and did not feel like she was in hard luck at all. She bragged, "We have a steam-heated room, plenty of eats, a good soft bed all cozy and comfortable."[122]

They started to see things differently as the months wore on. Prosecutors expected Jessie and Pearl to give evidence in exchange for their release once withdrawal symptoms started, but the sisters were not addicts. Instead, it was boredom and the desire to see their recently returned husbands that changed their minds. They were no longer laughing off the idea of jail time. By the time they raised their $25,000 bond, Jessie and Pearl never wanted to see the inside of a jail again. They would do whatever it took to remain free, including testifying against the Nolens.[123]

Chapter 9
BAD INFLUENCES

If you choose bad companions, no one will believe
that you are anything but bad yourself.
—Aesop, Aesop's Fables

Heat waves shimmered off the sidewalk in the sticky air. Streetcars rattled and hummed down South Main Street, squeaking to a halt at their stops. Passengers fanned themselves and tried to find seats in the shade. Cars parked here and there along the street in front of private apartments and businesses like Russell-Heckle Seed Company, Dunbar Molasses and Syrup Company and Sunshine Sales Company. Every conversation began with a comment about the heat. It seemed like a typical sunny July day until the police arrived.

The owners of the Banks Grocery on the first floor gawked as three Memphis police officers and two detectives jumped from their cars and surrounded their nondescript two-story building. Some covered the rear exit, while the others ran upstairs to 422½ South Main. Armed with short-barreled twelve-gauge shotguns, the officers kicked in the door. They found R.E. Wilson, a thirty-five-year-old gambler from Bisbee, Arizona; Dominick Masino, a cook from Tulsa; thirty-five-year-old James "Tip" O'Neal, twenty-nine-year-old Ethel Wikoff; and her boyfriend, Diggs Nolen.

O'Neal and his friends had been on a robbery spree when they blasted open the safe at the post office in Humboldt, Tennessee, the previous night. They escaped, but police identified O'Neal from the burglary tools left in his

South Main Street, south of Beale. *Courtesy of Memphis Public Library and Information Center.*

abandoned getaway car. Police then tracked the gang to Ethel's apartment in Memphis.[124]

Ethel, Diggs and three wanted bank robbers laughed when detectives crashed through the door. They had a quart of crème de menthe, a quart of Kentucky bourbon and two quarts of absinthe Ethel purchased from a Chicago hotel—all very illegal in Tennessee because of statewide prohibition. They had been lounging around the apartment quite drunk without a worry in the world until the detectives' unwelcome entrance announced the end of their party. Staring down the barrels of riot guns, the four men and the attractive brunette grinned and raised their hands.[125]

O'Neal and his friends struggled to give alibis. The eyes of the station officials bulged when Sergeant Joe Fitzgerald began counting the money he took from the arrested men. Fitzgerald found gold coins, banknotes and assorted change coming to over $5,000. Wilson had a thousand-dollar banknote folded in his pocket like a handkerchief. To make matters worse for the thieves, Massino could not hide his injuries from the nitroglycerin explosion during the robbery.

Attorney Charles M. Bryan convinced police to drop charges against Diggs. Though in the company of the robbers, Diggs had not played a part in their crimes. Officers turned O'Neal, Wilson and Masino over to federal authorities and charged Ethel with operating a disorderly house. The charge applied to anyone causing a disturbance; however, "disorderly house" frequently meant a place of prostitution. Unflustered by the insult, Ethel pulled out a one-hundred-dollar bill from the roll of cash in her handbag to pay the fifty-dollar forfeit required for her court appearance.[126]

Judge Lewis Fitzhugh fined Ethel another twenty-five dollars for violating the state prohibition law. Fortunately for Ethel, her arresting officer, R.D. Briggs, had served part of a term in the Shelby County Workhouse for petit larceny when he was nineteen. Commissioner Charles Quinn recruited Briggs, thinking the court had cleared the young man's record. Fitzhugh discovered the officer's criminal record and rendered him infamous and unable to testify in court. As a result, the judge dropped Ethel's charges.[127]

Diggs Nolen began seeing Ethel Wikoff again after his return from Leavenworth, but she was not his only love interest. He spent much of his time with a new girlfriend, Madelyn O'Reilly. Diggs and Madelyn tried to marry, but Madelyn had not finalized her divorce from her first husband. The two called off the marriage but remained friendly. Ethel eclipsed Madelyn as she began demanding more of Diggs's attention. Diggs, however, remained reluctant to commit to anyone again until Ethel threatened to marry another man. Giving in to jealousy, Diggs married Ethel on August 1, 1919.[128]

Ideally, Diggs and Ethel would have kept a low profile to avoid drawing attention to their illicit enterprises, but the young couple enjoyed the spotlight their newfound wealth brought them in the city's social circles. They hobnobbed and threw parties for both the city's elite and its underworld characters at their home at 393 North Garland. With his wife's encouragement, Diggs began acting as a go-between for thieves in the South and underworld characters in the North, as well as providing sanctuary and legal assistance to well-known outlaws, including Hart Austin.[129]

Police detective Lieutenant Lee Quianthy remembered Hart Austin as "just about as tough as any man I ever ran up against. He'd shoot it out with anybody living, no matter what the odds were." Austin and his gang targeted small country banks in Arkansas and Tennessee in the first weeks of 1920, and in February, he turned his sights on the People's Bank of Collierville. Austin needed to learn about the bank, so he posed as a representative of the National Bankers' Association investigating a forged check written by a young man who lived just across the state line in Mississippi. While speaking with a clerk, he followed her into the office next to the vault and asked questions about bank security. Meanwhile, Charles R. Anderson posed as a burglar alarm salesman to take a look at the vault and the layout of the bank.[130]

Austin and Anderson broke into a nearby blacksmith shop that night and stole a crowbar, hammer and chisel. They returned to the bank with two more cohorts shortly before sunrise and used the tools to break the padlock on the back door. They snuck in the back door and poured just enough nitroglycerin into the inner and outer vault door locks to blow them open without causing excessive damage. Once in the vault, the robbers ransacked the safe deposit boxes and stole money, jewelry and unregistered Liberty bonds.[131]

Austin needed to get rid of the stolen jewelry and bonds quickly, so he approached Diggs Nolen for help. Diggs fenced stolen goods for local thieves by selling them to mobsters in New York City, so liquidating the jewelry was easy. Selling stolen bonds, on the other hand, was something new. Diggs needed to find local buyers quickly, so he looked to people in his new social circles. Many of his new friends in the city's elite found him alluring because of his reputed underworld ties. Diggs turned on his charm and coaxed a lawyer and three prominent businessmen into buying the stolen bonds. The move made Diggs a hero in Austin's eyes, but it would also haunt Diggs until his final days.[132]

Within a year of his release from prison, Diggs Nolen went from having almost nothing to becoming both a successful businessman and a criminal kingpin. Rumors of Diggs's underworld activities brought increased scrutiny from law enforcement, but he was having too much fun to care. He continued to defy the law and thumb his nose at authority. He may have gotten away with it for a while, but the impish outlaw made a grave mistake: he got involved in politics.

Chapter 10
ROWLETT PAINE

It should not be possible for men the stripe of Diggs Nolen to give a shot of dope to the derelicts he controls and send them to the polls.
—*Rowlett Paine, November 7, 1919*

I'm not much for these church folks," Diggs Nolen told the reporter. "They wouldn't give me a square deal in my business. I'll stand all right with Mr. Williams. I've been promised that by men who know what they're talking about." Diggs thought his pharmacy business would do so well under the administration of J.J. Williams that he planned to give $600 to the former mayor's reelection campaign. Furthermore, he boasted, "I've got 150 dope friends, every one of them registered, the men with their poll taxes paid, and [I] am going to vote every one of them for Williams."[133]

An endorsement from Diggs Nolen was the last thing John Joseph "J.J." Williams needed. The former mayor, whom Memphians once hailed as a progressive because of his annexation efforts, had fallen into disfavor because he appeared soft on crime. He now faced fierce opposition from a group of reform-minded businessmen called the Citizens' League. The league endorsed a young grocer named J. Rowlett Paine as the answer to Williams, whom they cast as a throwback to the days of graft, cronyism and backroom deals with criminals. Edward Crump's favored candidate, William Bacon, dropped out of the race in September, leaving Paine and Williams in a heated campaign against each other. The Paine campaign seized on Diggs's endorsement and used it as evidence of collusion between Williams and the underworld. With the election only weeks away, Williams

Left: Mayor J.J. Williams. *Courtesy of Memphis Public Library and Information Center.*

Right: Mayor J. Rowlett Paine, circa 1924. *Courtesy of Memphis Public Library and Information Center.*

desperately needed to clean up his image—or, at the very least, save it from further damage.[134]

Diggs wanted to portray himself as a legitimate businessman, but Memphians were suspicious of his near monopoly on filling prescriptions for addicts from the police surgeon. The city's growing business elite valued and encouraged the quest for wealth and respectability, but they also encouraged traditional conservative values that Diggs seemed to lack. They saw drug users as criminals and degenerates rather than victims and looked down on any efforts to help them. Newspaper stories about Diggs's antics did not help his image either.[135]

Furthermore, Diggs did not realize that under Tennessee law, he could not possess a poll tax receipt or voter registration certificate belonging to another person. On October 26, 1919, Sheriff Oliver Perry and Deputy Edgar Harris raided the Crown Pharmacy in response to Diggs's boast. Perry seized ninety-three registration certificates, over thirty poll tax receipts and a handgun. Perry locked them in his office safe for state attorney general Sam O. Bates, while the Shelby County Grand Jury indicted Diggs for unlawful possession of registration certificates and carrying a pistol.[136]

Diggs's arrest provided more ammunition against Williams. The Paine campaign accused Diggs of attracting several hundred "dope fiends," run out of the city by police, back to Memphis and bribing them with drugs to vote for Williams. They claimed the scheme was part of the "same old rotten schemes to corrupt the ballot and debauch the election." Their campaign advertisements showed Diggs's arrest as evidence of a conspiracy to steal the election and turn the city over to criminals. They asked, "Why do such creatures back the Williams ticket?"[137]

The "Vote Williams for Mayor" banner flapped on the side of Diggs Nolen's car as he headed up Main Street. Diggs was soaking in the excitement of the election and the better part of a half-pint of whiskey. He took another sip to cut the chill of the evening air while he waved and shouted support for Williams to the people he passed.

Diggs looked up in time to swerve around a traffic cop at the corner of Monroe Avenue. The officer yelled at him. He yelled back. Diggs's face turned red, and he slammed on the brakes. He jumped from the car and

Main Street, downtown Memphis, circa 1912. *Courtesy of Memphis Public Library and Information Center.*

charged the officer. Traffic came to a standstill, and a crowd gathered to watch the brawl in the intersection.[138]

Diggs's car, as if it had a mind of its own and wanted nothing to do with the affair, continued up the street. Diggs had forgotten to take it out of gear. Drivers swerved, tires squealed and horns blew. The driverless vehicle drifted into oncoming traffic and directly toward the car of Joe Neutzel, the owner of a local bookbinding company. Its doomed journey ended with a smack and the sound of crunching metal and breaking glass.[139]

Mrs. S.H. Phillips recounted the scene to a crowd of over five hundred people at a Paine campaign rally at Forrest Park, describing how she nearly collided with Diggs's car. Phillips added, "I telephoned police headquarters a few minutes ago and Diggs had been released on bond. Conditions such as those should not be permitted in Memphis. The laws must be enforced regardless of who the violators support politically."[140]

Diggs had played into the hands of Williams's enemies and helped Rowlett Paine and the other Citizens' League candidates win the election. Diggs motivated voters, already dissatisfied with factional politics and corruption, to defeat Williams by over 2,700 votes. Paine's campaign team thanked the staff of the *News Scimitar* for their support and offered "the kindliest feelings" for Williams, whom they called a pleasant and affable gentleman. They blamed the mayor's defeat on "the crowd that lined up with him" and singled out Diggs as carrying the most blame.[141]

Diggs found himself on the wrong side of the newspapers, the new mayor and law enforcement. On January 17, 1920, Inspector William D.

Jamaica Ginger advertisement. *Courtesy of Library of Congress.*

Bee arrested Diggs for violating the National Prohibition Act by selling Jamaican Ginger, a high-alcohol tonic, in unmarked bottles. Two days later, a federal narcotics agent named C.A. Woods copied the serial numbers from ten- and five-dollar bills and gave them to a stool pigeon to purchase drugs from Diggs. The addict made the purchase, left the store and turned over the evidence to U.S. deputy marshal Bert Bates. At six o'clock in the afternoon, Bates and Sheriff Perry raided Diggs's pharmacy. Bates arrested Diggs, who still had the recorded bills, while Perry seized narcotics from the pharmacy. Diggs was held for three hours until he posted a $1,000 bond.[142]

In March 1920, Diggs found himself on the wrong side of his wife. Neighbors heard Diggs and Ethel fighting at their home at 393 North Garland. Several gunshots rang out, and Diggs stumbled out the door to the back porch, clutching his leg. Diggs called to his cousin, "Floyd, don't let her shoot me anymore!" A bullet had entered just above the knee, fractured the bone and lodged just below the skin on the opposite side.[143]

Police inspector Mike Kehoe arrested Ethel for attempted murder as doctors admitted Diggs to the hospital. Diggs hoped to save Ethel from prosecution and himself from embarrassment by lying about how he was shot. First, Diggs claimed he shot himself when he dropped his gun while cleaning it. He later claimed someone wounded him in a duel. Ethel, still too angry to appreciate his chivalry, filed for divorce in circuit court on June 25.[144]

Meanwhile, Diggs's trial stemming from his arrest for narcotics in January resulted in a hung jury. Mistrials had become common as federal courts were stymied by confusion about new liquor and narcotics laws and the legality of search warrants. Even if the jury had convicted Diggs, his case would likely have been tied up in the federal appeals court in Cincinnati for years because of the backlog of new prohibition cases.[145]

Diggs's trial resulting from the November drug bust in Little Rock came up before Judge Trieber on June 16. Diggs, still on crutches, represented himself and denied knowledge of the drug transaction involving Jessie Cannoy, Pearl Hunt and his cousin Floyd Diggs. Even with the cooperation of the sisters, the jury could not reach a unanimous decision. Once again, Diggs was free because of a mistrial.[146]

Floyd Nolen, however, pleaded guilty to his part in the conspiracy. The judge sentenced him to two years at the Atlanta Federal Prison and fined him $2,000. Trieber, however, relented after a tearful plea from Floyd's wife and reduced the sentence to one year and a day and the fine to $500.[147]

Federal district attorney William Kyser, frustrated by his inability to convict Diggs, found a new angle when the collector of internal revenue notified him that Diggs had not paid any taxes for 1918 and 1919. In addition, Diggs's taxes had increased because of the high volume of narcotics prescriptions he filled over the previous year. On June 19, Kyser filed a lien against the pharmacist for tax evasion for just over

U.S. district attorney William Kyser. *Courtesy of Memphis Public Library and Information Center.*

$47,000. If Kyser could not put Diggs in jail, he would hit him with a heavy fine instead.[148]

Newspaper editor C.P.J. Mooney recommended that Diggs hire John E. McCall Jr., son of the recently deceased federal judge, to appeal his case. Diggs did not keep books, so McCall had to examine every receipt over the previous two years. After several months, McCall negotiated the penalty down to $6,000. The case was closed, or so he thought.[149]

The irate IRS agent who filed the initial charges against Diggs filed more charges without informing McCall. Diggs could have paid the fine out of pocket, but he instead reached out to his underworld contacts in New York for help. His connections in the Big Apple presented a scheme that would not only allow Diggs to come up with the money to settle the fine but also provide a handsome profit.[150]

Chapter II

LIBERTY BONDS

Yesterday a man called me on the phone about 6 o'clock saying he was Nolen,
and asked me if I sold his bonds to Priddy-Williams. I told him no, that I had
sold them through A.K. Tigrett and Company, and asked him why.
He said, "Have you read the morning paper?" and hung up.
—John McCall Jr., February 5, 1921

Liberty bonds were debt obligations issued by the U.S. Department of the Treasury in conjunction with the Federal Reserve in four installments between 1917 and 1918 to finance the war effort in Europe. Those who invested in these bonds would receive their money back, plus interest, after a certain number of years. The government propaganda effort under George Creel organized a massive public awareness campaign using posters, billboards and celebrity endorsements. The fifth and final release of Liberty bonds in April 1919 was called "Victory Bonds" in celebration of the war's end.[151]

Under Secretary of the Treasury William McAdoo, the bonds were made negotiable, with coupons cashable every six months. The government did not want to deal with the administrative cost of tracking ownership, so it designated Liberty bonds as "bearer bonds." These are securities that belong to whoever is holding them at the time rather than one registered owner.

Most Americans could not afford the fifty-dollar bonds, so McAdoo introduced twenty-five-cent War Thrift Stamps. The buyer could exchange a sixteen-stamp book for a five-dollar War Savings Stamp. The buyer would

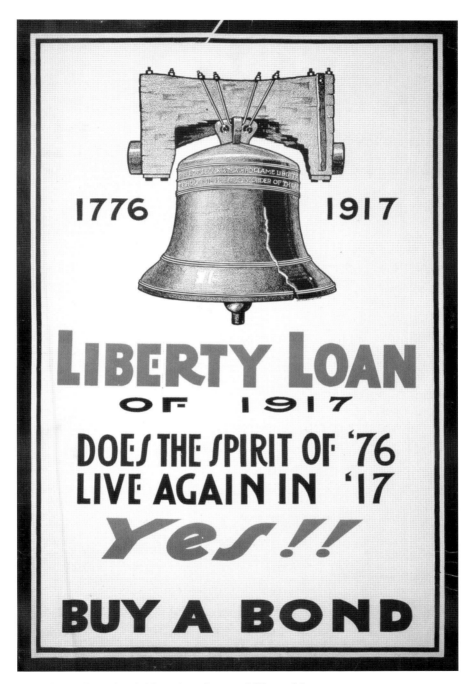

Poster from Liberty bond drive, 1917. *Courtesy of Library of Congress.*

then attach five War Savings Stamps to an interest-earning War Savings Certificate. Ten certificates were converted into a fifty-dollar Liberty bond. Unlike the bearer bonds, a certificate could be cashed only by the person named on it.

Even so, Liberty bonds became very tempting targets for thieves. Each had a serial number for identification, but there were so many Liberty bonds sold and so many stolen that many assumed the government could not keep track of them all. Thieves counted on the difficulty of tracking stolen Liberty bonds to make them almost as safe to negotiate as banknotes.[152]

Brooklyn, New York City, November 1920

Tony Vanelli and two of his crew were doing an awful job of being inconspicuous. The gangsters in fancy suits stood by a fence and shuffled around to keep warm. Workers unloading trucks at Igoe Brothers factory across the street could not help but notice them. Fifteen-year-old Sophie Zowyski studied the young men from her doorstep up the block. She wondered why a flashy bunch of guys would be hanging around this drab working-class section of the Williamsburg neighborhood in Brooklyn, New York, on a Tuesday afternoon.

Vanelli, also known as Antonio Santini or simply the Chief, was the head of the Canine Club, a gang of hoodlums headquartered in an East Eleventh Street barbershop in Manhattan. The hardest work the Bronx native had done since his release from Sing Sing on a burglary rap had been "to persuade a pair of dice to do his bidding." He wore swanky clothes and expensive jewelry and carried a fat roll of money in his pocket. The craps-shooting Vanelli did not so much as walk as stroll from one of his haunts to another with bored indifference and a cigarette dangling from his lip.

That morning, Canine Club member Joey Degregario gave Vanelli some welcome news. His brother Tony Degregario, the supervisor of the couriers for Irving Cohen of the Kean, Taylor and Company bond brokers in Manhattan, had just dispatched two unarmed young men carrying $466,000 worth of mostly unregistered Liberty bonds. Vanelli, his friend Joseph Amurso and two other gangsters left the barbershop to track down the couriers.[153]

Twenty-nine-year-old Austin Young and twenty-one-year-old Irving Cohen headed to the Igoe Brothers office across the East River in

Williamsburg. The company manufactured nails, rivets, wire, reinforcing steel and fencing. The couriers thought it was just another routine delivery. Neither had any idea of the contents of the locked cowhide bag.[154]

Young notified Igoe Brothers by telephone of the delivery. At noon, the couriers took the Broadway Subway from Chambers Street in Manhattan over the Williamsburg Bridge to the Marcy Station in Brooklyn. Young and Cohen took turns carrying the satchel as they walked ten blocks north to 69–73 Metropolitan Avenue. They saw seven trucks with drivers and crews waiting by the loading docks as they turned the corner. They also noticed the men across the street from the factory.[155]

The gangsters waited for the right moment. Once their targets got close enough, they hid their faces under their hats and rushed them. A blow to his head from a blackjack brought Cohen to his knees. Vanelli jammed his pistol in Young's side and ordered him to let go of the bag. Young refused and held on as the robbers grabbed him by the neck and dragged him to the ground.[156]

A shot rang out. Young dropped the bag and reached for the side of his head where the bullet had grazed his left ear. The bandits turned and ran up the street toward the waiting getaway car at the corner of Wythe. Vanelli snatched the courier's satchel and followed his friends as Young and some of the Igoe workers chased after him. Vanelli could hear his pursuers closing in, but before they could grab him, a shot from his pistol sent the men diving for cover.

Vanelli sprinted to the car and jumped on the running board. The engine roared to life, and the Chief held tight with his free hand. The driver turned the car toward Broadway. Hanging on to the side of the speeding Ford, Vanelli fired more shots in the air to deter any more would-be pursuers.[157]

Vanelli had just pulled off the biggest robbery in New York City in over a year. Now he had to figure out what to do with his prize. There was no way he could sell over $400,000 in stolen bonds alone without being arrested, and he could not keep the bonds either, since every cop in the city was looking for them. He needed help to get rid of them, and he needed it fast.

In December, Peter Duffy met with Diggs Nolen during a trip to Memphis to sell narcotics and fake government whiskey labels. The Hell's Kitchen gangster liked Diggs, so he gladly obliged when his Memphis connection asked for help. Duffy told Diggs that he could set him up with a cache of stolen Liberty bonds to liquidate for a generous profit. Diggs eagerly accepted the offer, since he had so easily sold the bonds Hart Austin stole earlier in the year.[158]

One of Vanelli's associates, simply known as "Yinkie," had approached Duffy and James Carroll in Manhattan about selling the stolen bonds. Yinkie gave them the first $750 in bonds at a coffeehouse on Thompson Street, promising more if they could sell the first batch. Duffy sold the first bonds in Washington, D.C., and returned for more. He assured Yinkie that he knew a guy in Memphis, a "real straight-shooter," that could dispose of the rest of the bonds. With Yinkie's approval, Duffy and chauffeurs Frank Goldberg and Jacob K. Rosenberg took the bonds to Memphis.[159]

On January 7, 1921, police officers on the lookout for shady characters arrested Duffy and Goldberg near the Crown Pharmacy. The gangsters had just delivered the bonds to Diggs, so the two were carrying only empty suitcases and a pint of whiskey. Duffy and Goldberg could not explain why they had come to town or why they were hanging around the pharmacy. The officers sensed the two were up to something and held them for suspicious behavior and liquor violations. Diggs posted bond for the men later that evening, and both jumped bail and left town. The arrest seemed insignificant at the time, but it was the first in a series of mistakes that would come back to haunt Diggs.[160]

Diggs Nolen could not sell the Liberty bonds alone, so he formed a ring of trusted coconspirators to help. He first reached out to his lawyer, John McCall. When he got the call, McCall thought that Diggs wanted to discuss his case. Instead, Diggs asked for help selling some bonds to cover his legal fees. McCall assumed the sales were legitimate, so he sold $100,000 in bonds to A.K. Tigrett and Company to cover his costs and Diggs's fine.[161]

Diggs also asked the help of Maurice Joseph of Joseph Myers Jewelers, R.E. Priddy of Priddy-Williams bond dealers and James Money Vardaman of the Bank of Commerce, son of former United States senator James Vardaman of Mississippi. Diggs then recruited City National Bank vice president William L. Huntley Jr., whose family had close ties to the Nolens in Mississippi, and Holloway Gang member R.A. Graham, who specialized in forgery and confidence scams. Of the $350,000 in bonds that came to Memphis, Huntley sold $65,000 to Union Planters Bank and Trust, and Graham, under the alias "Mr. Cameron," sold another $110,000 to the same bank. They sold the remainder to unsuspecting bankers in Clarksdale, Birmingham, Atlanta and New Orleans.[162]

Union Planters Bank and Trust, downtown Memphis office. *Courtesy of Memphis Public Library and Information Center.*

Diggs counted on bankers not checking the registration numbers, but the high profile of the Igoe Brothers robbery had banks on alert for any suspicious transactions. In late January, C.F. Childs and Company of Chicago representatives sent $90,000 in bonds to the Federal Reserve Bank for transfer into smaller denominations. Regulators spotted the stolen bonds and discovered that they came to Chicago by way of the Union Planters Bank in Memphis.[163]

Rather than keep a low profile, Diggs and his friends routinely flashed large amounts of money around the city. Huntley and the Nolens sold $255,000 in bonds and cashed another $100,000. Ethel then tried to change a $10,000 bill, and Jacob Rosenberg paid a year's rent for a new apartment in advance, an unusual move for someone with such a low-paying job. The chauffeur caused even greater suspicion when he gave Diggs as a reference.[164]

It was not long before suspicious bankers notified police of the unusual transactions of Diggs and his friends. Once Memphis police inspector Will Griffin confirmed the bonds came from the New York heist, Huntley promptly resigned from his bank, and James Vardaman was suspended from his bank pending investigation. Police arrested Duffy in Washington, D.C., and Vanelli surrendered on February 10 in New York.[165]

Huntley claimed he thought the sale was legitimate and acted on behalf of a person named Bradley Anderson. The U.S. Department of Justice and six private detective agencies assisted in a nationwide search for Anderson, to no avail. Anderson, also known as Andy "Slim" Anderson, remained at large until November 1925, when he died in a running gun battle with the police following a clothing store robbery in Raleigh, North Carolina.[166]

Inspector Griffin arrested Diggs and Ethel Nolen and charged them with larceny and receiving stolen goods. Griffin added a bribery charge against Ethel when she offered him $50 to drop the charges. Diggs was too drunk to appear in court and was left in a cell until he sobered up. He was released a couple of days later on a $10,000 bail, and Ethel was released on a $5,000 bail. Two weeks later, the Shelby County Grand Jury returned indictments against the Nolens and their friends. Huntley and the others feared Diggs's notoriety might influence a jury's decision, so they asked to be tried separately.[167]

The last piece of the prosecution's case fell into place with the capture of Peter Duffy. Investigators made the connection between Duffy and Diggs after learning of the January arrest of Duffy and Goldberg in Memphis. In Washington, D.C., Duffy bragged that he was the only one involved in the heist to get away and promised to "shoot the first cop who tried to flush him." In March, police arrested Duffy after a brief foot chase through the streets. Duffy dropped the bravado during his interrogation and admitted that he delivered the stolen bonds to Diggs. When marshals brought him back to Memphis, Duffy announced, "Here I am, and I'm willing to tell all I know concerning those stolen bonds."[168]

Chapter 12

ETHEL WIKOFF

Heaven has no rage like love to hatred turned,
nor Hell a fury like a woman scorned.
—*William Congreve,* The Mourning Bride

Diggs Nolen and his chauffer Sonny Owens arrived at the Crown Pharmacy shortly after midnight and found Ethel waiting behind the pharmacy counter. She was angry, and Diggs was drunk, so Owens thought it best to leave the two alone. From the next room, Owens heard the two shouting and cursing each other. They began to scuffle, and Ethel screamed, "Take your hands off that pistol!" A shot rang out, and Diggs fell to the floor, begging, "Please, don't shoot me anymore!" The front door flew open, and Ethel, with her head held high and all her jewels shaking and glittering like an angry Christmas tree, marched out of the pharmacy as the sirens closed in.[169]

The J.T. Hinton and Son ambulance crew found Diggs reeking of booze, barely coherent and bleeding badly where the bullet had entered to the right of his navel. The looks on the stretcher-bearer's faces made his spirits sink. He asked, "Will I beat it? Will I live?" At one o'clock in the morning, Dr. Joseph E. Johnson performed surgery to stitch Diggs's liver. Hovering between life and death, Diggs looked as though he would not make it through the night.[170]

During the preceding weeks, the indictments caused the tension between Diggs and Ethel to reach a boiling point. Rather than work things out with his wife, Diggs went on a bender. Police arrested him seven times for public drunkenness in the two weeks following his indictments. After his release from the drunk tank, Diggs came home eager to get even with Ethel for giving him a black eye during a recent fight. Diggs stormed into the house and began beating Ethel. She fought her way free of his grip, fled in her nightclothes to her mother's house and left the next day for Chicago.[171]

Ethel returned to Memphis on February 20 after the Shelby County Grand Jury indicted her for bribery. That evening, she shot Diggs and fled the scene. Facing a possible murder charge, Ethel consulted with her attorney, Charles M. Bryan. The next day, she took Bryan's advice, surrendered to Sheriff Oliver Perry and claimed self-defense.[172]

While Diggs lay in the hospital, J.N. Robinson of the local IRS office issued a distress warrant to hold Diggs's property to cover his delinquent taxes. Attorney John McCall had anticipated the move and instructed Diggs to close his bank account, call in his collateral and give his pharmacy to his father ahead of the warrant. As the case stalled, the IRS agreed to allow Diggs and Ernest to manage the store until they could pay the back taxes or sell the property.[173]

Ernest Nolen took control of managing the pharmacy while his brother lay in the hospital, but Ethel, expecting to be widowed, believed she was entitled to the pharmacy. She stole the door keys and threatened to kill Ernest if he tried to take them back. The IRS sent U.S. marshals to the store to protect Ernest, while Ethel countered by telling Captain Will Lee of the police department that Ernest threatened to "clean out the whole Wikoff family."[174]

Just as the situation neared violence, Diggs made a surprise recovery, defying predictions he would not survive through the night. The surgeon, satisfied with Diggs's return to health, decided not to operate and left the bullet in Diggs's abdomen. The following morning, he told reporters, "His chances are good. He is on the mend fast." By the afternoon, Diggs was sitting up in bed, drinking eggnog and smoking cigarettes.[175]

Thunderstorms pounded the Shelby County Courthouse as Diggs Nolen, still limping badly, entered the courtroom with his mother and brother. The judge had delayed Diggs's trial while he recovered, and during that time, defense attorneys had time to discover a technical error in the charges. In court, lawyers for Diggs Nolen and William L. Huntley Jr. pointed out that the charges stated the bonds were the possession of the Igoe Brothers, but

Shelby County Courthouse entrance. *Courtesy of Memphis Public Library and Information Center.*

the second charge stated Austin Young had possession of the bonds. The Huntleys' lawyer, P.J. Lyons, asked for a directed verdict of not guilty because the documents were unclear about who had possession of the bonds at the time of the robbery.[176]

The judge overruled the motion but did not resolve the question. The jury had the case from 5:00 p.m. Monday until 10:35 the following morning. During that time, the jurors could not get an answer from the prosecutor regarding whether a guilty verdict would stand with the unclear verbiage.[177]

The next morning, Huntley and Diggs, both showing the strain of the lengthy trial, watched closely as jury foreman Fred Haydel passed the verdict to court clerk Mike Cohen. Cohen read, "We, the jury, find the defendants not guilty." The jury members, without clear directions regarding the unclear verbiage, did not feel they could convict. Huntley began clapping, but Judge Richards rapped it down. Huntley's family ran to the jurors to shake their hands, and Huntley's Irish father-in-law grasped the hand of his friend C.J. Kehoe and exclaimed, "Sinn Fein!"[178]

Diggs and McCall faced a second indictment, but there was little chance of conviction. The cases against the other men indicted fell apart as well. The Shelby County Grand Jury ignored the larceny and receiving stolen goods charges against Ethel and dismissed the bribery charge. Shelby County attorney general Sam O. Bates had to admit that he and his team had blown the case.[179]

Diggs and Ethel could now focus on resolving their differences. The judge held over Ethel's court date for assault to murder until June 7, 1921. Diggs kept his distance from her and stayed at the Adler Hotel following his discharge from the hospital. Each had threatened the other with divorce, but both realized that a court battle would expose their criminal activities and land them in jail. Each one waited for the other to make the first move.[180]

Ethel's penchant for shooting Diggs gave him cause to want to divorce her, but a new woman in his life gave him reason to follow through. While in the hospital, Diggs struck up a friendship with a twenty-six-year-old nurse named Margaret May Haring. After his discharge, their friendship turned into a romantic relationship. Diggs, fearing the possible wrath of his gun-toting wife, sued for divorce citing cruel and inhuman treatment in May 1921. Diggs claimed Ethel was of such a violent temper and so frequent in her assaults that it was no longer safe to live with her.[181]

Judge Ben Capell granted Diggs's divorce application. Ethel's attorney, Charles M. Bryan, and Diggs's attorney, Ralph Davis, conferred and recommended their clients take no further action. Any public difference between them would certainly bring to light their criminal escapades, and this was certainly not the time to allow public knowledge of any of their conspiracies. Bryan and Davis cautioned their clients that Memphians had lost patience with them and begun pressuring local law enforcement to find a way to rid the city of the troublesome couple.[182]

Chapter 13

OLIVER PERRY

Diggs Nolen is a trafficker in soul-destroying drugs and a promoter of crime.
—Sheriff Oliver Hazard Perry, September 1921

Diggs Nolen took a new interest in life in the spring of 1921. He had a budding romance with Margaret Haring, and his health had returned. He bought a new Cadillac Six Touring Car and drove it to city parks every day, where fresh air and exercise helped him recover from his gunshot wound. IRS deputy collector J.S. Robinson found that auditors had overestimated Diggs's income, so he settled the claim against Diggs, released the Crown Pharmacy back to him and voided the distress warrants. Diggs thought he was going to get a fresh start, but he failed to realize the extent of the resentment the public had toward him. Those feelings came to a head in the summer, when an event set in motion an effort to rid the city of Diggs once and for all.[183]

On August 10, 1921, Ford Motor Company clerk Edward McHenry and security guards Howard Gamble and Polk Carraway rode back from the bank with $8,500 for payroll. As the three parked in front of the Ford Motor Company Plant on Union Avenue, armed bandits pulled up next to them and demanded the money. Gunfire erupted, killing Gamble and Carraway. McHenry stumbled out of the car as bullets flew around him and bolted for the building with the money. As sirens approached, the bandits sped away empty-handed.[184]

Roadblocks went up around the city manned by nervous deputies ready for gunplay. In Collierville, just east of Memphis, Lieutenant Vincent Lucarini waved his uniform hat to identify himself as he drove up to a roadblock, but Morris Irby, the deputy in charge, did not understand the signal. The posse opened fire, killed Lucarini and wounded his deputized assistants Joseph Robilio, Edward Heckinger and C.L. Bonds.[185]

The Ford Motor Company robbery was latest in a series of sensational crimes. Frustrated by the ineffectiveness of law enforcement, the chamber of commerce called a mass meeting of civic and labor organizations to mobilize against the crime wave. A group of two hundred people calling themselves the Vigilantes met at the Lyric Theater and made plans to hunt down undesirables and shut down "festering places of crime." They chose to launch their campaign by targeting the city's highest-profile criminal, Diggs Nolen. Sheriff Oliver Perry and other law enforcement officials turned their sights on Diggs to appease the group. After the robbery, police arrested Diggs on charges of drunkenness, carrying a pistol and selling narcotics.[186]

Diggs had recently attracted the attention of the Prohibition Bureau as well. In June 1921, he briefly relocated to the Arkansas oil boomtown El Dorado and started a pharmacy as a cover for a bootlegging operation. Diggs advertised in the local newspaper that he wanted a partner with $5,000 to invest. He wrote, "No chance to fail on making big money in this with me." El Dorado residents did not know the identity of the partner, but rumors circulated that Ethel had taken up the offer in hopes of reconciling with Diggs.[187]

Prohibition agents made sure Diggs's bootlegging operation never got off the ground. In July, Agent Louis Elkins shut down the Chisca Chemical Company at 344 Poplar Avenue after the sale of ten gallons of nonbeverage alcohol to Diggs without a permit. In August, Marshal Arthur Ellis arrested four of Diggs's bootleggers near Camden, Arkansas, and dumped their cargo in the city sewer.[188]

Meanwhile, Memphis police focused on Diggs's narcotics operation. Inspector Will Griffin and a team of ten detectives raided the Crown Pharmacy in July 1921 and arrested Diggs and George Goodnow, a.k.a. New York George, after Goodnow purchased morphine from one of Diggs's clerks with the intent to sell. Police arrested Diggs while he was out on bond for selling morphine to a police informer named H.B. Dezonia. After his release on bond, Diggs tracked down Dezonia, beat him up and threatened to kill him. The addict then showed more wisdom than courage and left town. Once prosecutors realized their witness would never return, they had no other choice but to eventually drop the case in March 1922.[189]

The Vigilantes began making threats against Diggs after his release. Fearing the mob would come after him, Diggs asked Sheriff Oliver Perry to take him into protective custody. Perry took the opportunity to charge Diggs with breach of peace, a charge that allowed Perry to keep Diggs locked up indefinitely for being a threat to public safety. Diggs tried to use habeas corpus to gain his release, but Perry would only release Diggs if he left Memphis for good. On September 3, 1921, Diggs gave in and signed the agreement over his attorney's protest.

> *I, Diggs Nolen, do hereby agree to close my drugstore at the corner of Main and Vance, known as the Crown Drugstore, within twenty days and do hereby agree not to own any part of the drugstore or any interest in same and do further agree to leave the city of Memphis and Shelby County within twenty days and never try to open drugstores in the city of Memphis.*

Diggs, however, lingered in Memphis. He claimed a week later that he tried to "sell out, but failed," so he placed the Crown Pharmacy in receivership under the control of Joe Marks. Marks liquidated the business's assets to pay all those to whom Diggs owed money. It was a kind of "time out," or protective umbrella, for the troubled pharmacy to avoid bankruptcy. The receiver stepped in to manage the business, its assets and all financial and operating decisions. While in receivership, Diggs remained in place as a material contributor with only limited authority.[190]

On September 16, 1921, Perry reluctantly admitted he could not run Diggs and Ernest out of Memphis after attorneys informed him that no official had such authority. The chastised sheriff explained to reporters that he could not "act as a czar" and exile anyone by "administrative process." Even so, he called Diggs a "trafficker in soul-destroying drugs and a promoter of crime" and promised to keep a careful watch on him.[191]

Diggs left his attorney to work with the receiver and departed for Rochester, Minnesota, to consult with a surgeon about the bullet still lodged in his abdomen. He felt confident that with the threat of exile lifted, he would return to Memphis, repair his tarnished reputation and get his pharmacy operational again. He had assets to cover his debts, and his only secured creditor was the National Cash Register Company, which held his cash register valued at $1,750. It was a small problem, but one that Diggs could easily fix, or so he thought.[192]

Chapter 14
WATERLOO

Nearly everything worthwhile to me depends
on this advertisement making an impression.
—Diggs Nolen, May 1922

Diggs Nolen's former girlfriend Madeline O'Reilly made the check out for $750. It was less than Diggs needed, but he could fix that. Just one little mark between the dollar sign and the seven would raise the amount by $1,000. Diggs needed the money quickly, because he would soon leave town for his wedding. Out of all the check-writing schemes Diggs had been involved in, altering this check seemed like a small risk. O'Reilly had loaned him money before; surely, she would overlook this one check. Diggs thought it over and decided to take the chance. He made the mark and cashed the check.

Diggs no longer worried about Sheriff Perry running him out of the city, but he was still struggling to get the Crown Pharmacy solvent again. Diggs was losing his customers and running out of money. Bankers refused to extend credit to him because of the headlines about his escapades and arrests. Diggs needed to change the minds of his former customers, so he decided to use the instrument that had turned them against him.

In May 1922, Diggs ran a page-long advertisement in the *Commercial Appeal* newspaper asking for the citizens of Memphis to give him a second chance. Diggs promised to run a "cut-rate" store with reduced prices, keep the store open twenty-four hours a day and provide a motorcycle delivery service.

He invited Memphians to write letters to him so that he could respond to each writer personally in hopes of overcoming the "prejudices existing in the minds of many."[193]

Diggs got his first feedback the next day. Like many Memphians in the 1920s, Diggs would offer rides in his car to people waiting for public transportation. On his way to work, he noticed a heavyset woman waiting for a streetcar at the corner of Cleveland and Poplar Avenue and offered to drive her downtown. The woman gladly accepted and sat down in the backseat of Diggs's Cadillac. Diggs exchanged pleasantries without introducing himself, and his passenger did not recognize him. She leaned back in the seat and began leafing through her copy of the Saturday morning newspaper.

The woman complained about the Memphis Streetcar Company and city services in general for the next five blocks until Diggs stopped to offer a ride to a young couple. The young man and woman climbed in and sat in the back, next to the woman with the paper. As they drove on, this woman reached Diggs's advertisement and mistook it for a news article. Her ire shifted to Diggs.

"I guess he's bought off the newspapers now," she griped.

The young woman quipped, "What office is he holding now?"

The young man boasted that he knew all about Diggs because he went to college with him. He argued with the women about Diggs's character and criminal record as Diggs listened quietly. He and the other passengers were dropped off at their destinations without any of them recognizing their driver.

Diggs wrote the following week, "When I dropped the three at Main and Madison, my career had been described, defamed, and lauded to quite an extent. I felt pretty blue when I reached the store. The fat lady's indictments kept recurring, and the young man's foolish ideas were disquieting."[194]

Diggs's first attempt to get people to change their minds about him had not gone as well as he had hoped. He ran a second advertisement thanking those who had written to him and boasting of his increase in sales. He complained that the Liberty bonds case had destroyed his credit, and he could not secure a loan because bank officials told him that public opinion was still against him.

Diggs made a veiled threat against the "powers that be." He claimed he "quit the underworld" but refused the U.S. Department of Justice's offers to work as a paid informant to expose those who helped him in his criminal endeavors, including the sale of the stolen Liberty bonds. "I state this to ease the minds of some of the elite," wrote Diggs. "For if I ever did start talking,

Madison Avenue, Memphis, circa 1919. *Courtesy of Memphis Public Library and Information Center.*

the draft for Atlanta and Nashville [Penitentiaries] would not be selective by any means. The top crust would be represented, as well as the underworld. Let the past be of no concern, however."[195]

On June 6, 1922, Diggs published his third letter thanking his supporters. The previous Saturday, he wrote, his staff delivered 144 packages, about three times his usual business. He had received over three hundred letters, and he promised to answer everyone.[196]

The police, unimpressed by Diggs's public relations campaign, stood ready to pounce at the slightest infraction. On June 17, 1922, police, armed with a search warrant, raided Diggs's parents' house at 52 North Tucker and seized a cache of narcotics purchased from the W.N. Wilkerson and Sons wholesale drug company. Officers found seventy-six one-eighth-ounce bottles of cocaine, seventy-three one-eighth-ounce bottles of diacetylmorphine, seventy-eight one-eighth-ounce bottles of morphine sulfate, five syringes and some unidentified pills. Each bottle was worth three dollars legitimately but one hundred dollars apiece on the black market. A week later, police arrested Diggs's father when he sold morphine to an unregistered addict at the Van Ray Pharmacy.[197]

Diggs responded to the raid on his father's house with a fourth letter. He claimed he'd been worried about a possible break-in at his pharmacy, so he moved the drugs for safekeeping until he could return the surplus drugs to the Wilkerson Brothers. The federal grand jury verified that Diggs held permits for the drugs; however, he had violated the conditions of the license terms by moving the drugs to his house.[198]

The news guaranteed no local banker would loan Diggs money. Unable to secure a bank loan, Diggs resorted to borrowing money from former girlfriend Madeline O'Reilly. Diggs used his old confidence scheme methods and struck up a friendship with the thirty-one-year-old divorcée again in the summer of 1922. She was financially well off, owned property off Horn Lake Road south of Memphis and had a soft spot for Diggs. O'Reilly was having a new home built on a lot in an upscale neighborhood on South Belvedere. Diggs frequently drove her to the property to check on the progress of construction. He flattered and flirted with her to gain her trust. Diggs lavished so much attention on her that he caused her contractor, who had romantic interests in her, to become jealous.[199]

O'Reilly wrote Diggs a check for $750 to help pay for his cash register. She had collected $196.50 from a previous loan when Diggs put his store in receivership, so she trusted he would pay her back. Diggs, however, altered the check before he cashed it. He added a number 1 before the 750 and raised the total to $1,750. O'Reilly was infuriated when she found out what Diggs had done and had him arrested.[200]

While out on bond, Diggs married Margaret May Haring at her parents' home in Butler, Ohio, on September 4, 1922. The happy occasion, however, was marred by the forgery charges. He returned to Memphis not happy and eager to start over but rather frustrated and eager to lash out at authority. Over the next few months, police arrested him on liquor charges, narcotics violations and weapons charges and for shooting and wounding a man.[201]

On December 8, 1922, Diggs appeared in court to face O'Reilly's forgery charges. He claimed he paid O'Reilly back $750 and gave her a predated check to cover the remainder. Diggs accused O'Reilly of acting out of spite. He said she wanted Diggs to move in with her and became jealous and pressed charges when she found out his new wife planned to return to Memphis.

O'Reilly, however, was no pushover. She was beautiful, charming, educated and financially independent. She was also tough enough to have fended off gunman Hart Austin when he tried to kill her in August 1921.

Diggs's attorney, Charles M. Bryan, asked questions about her personal life that would have embarrassed most women of the time, but O'Reilly stood her ground and deflected his accusations of impropriety.[202]

"[Diggs] has met his Waterloo," wrote a reporter when the jury sided with O'Reilly. Diggs had appeared in court many times over the previous few years but had yet to serve any jail time. That changed when the judge sentenced Diggs to three to fifteen years in the state penitentiary. "I was guilty of the narcotics charge, but I didn't forge any check," he insisted. Diggs continued to deny any wrongdoing years later, saying she filed the charges out of jealousy. He said of O'Reilly, "Oh, she was beautiful, but she was treacherous."[203]

Diggs's campaign to re-create his public image lay in ruins after the trial. More arrests followed for petty crimes in the days leading up to his sentencing. A local reporter wrote:

> In his meteoric course through the limitless and boundless space of local lawlessness, H. Diggs Nolen has bumped against the stone wall of all the courts and has engaged in encounters with many laws. His career is dotted with arrests, bonds, fines, narrow escapes, and narrower trials.... There was a time when the arrest of Diggs Nolen created a sort of sensation. It is no longer so. He has been arrested so much within the past two or three years that the public and press have come to consider it merely as a matter of course.[204]

Chapter 15
DRUGS, TARZAN AND BIRDS OF PARADISE

His life's history is written with the ink of accusation and the pen of scorn.
—*The* Commercial Appeal, *September 1922*

Diggs Nolen's world had come crashing down because of the fraud trial. He lost his sense of direction and faith in his ability to succeed as he sank deeper into addiction. Diggs's desperation to feed his growing morphine habit had made him willing to take greater risks to acquire money. Frustration over his failing business caused him to lash out at friends and foes alike. His lawyers tried to find legal loopholes to free him from his impending prison sentences, but Diggs did not make it easy for them. Every day outside of prison was another day Diggs got into trouble.

John Costicos stood sweating outside Ernest Nolen's Van Ray Pharmacy near Vance Avenue and Third Street. The thirty-one-year-old Greek immigrant had smuggled fifteen quarts of Canadian Club whisky and two birds of paradise from New Orleans. Costicos charged Diggs Nolen $96 for the liquor and $120 for the birds. Diggs gave him $6 with a promise to pay him the remainder.[205]

Now, on this muggy August morning, the Greek waited for Diggs to show up with the rest of the money owed. Instead of Diggs, however, police detectives Thompson, Quianthy and Fox showed up and arrested Costicos for bootlegging and trafficking stolen goods. Diggs surrendered the birds after detectives raided his parents' house.[206]

Diggs was out on bond in late September 1922 when he showed up drunk at Renegar's Café at Adams and Lauderdale. He made the mistake of picking a fight with nineteen-year-old prizefighter Herman Sanders, a.k.a. Al "Tarzan" Munro. The outmatched Diggs never stood a chance. After a brief skirmish, Munro threw a punch that knocked Diggs out.[207]

Munro and his father, fifty-year-old A.M. Sanders, left before Diggs woke up, but Diggs was determined to even the score. He got in his car and caught up with Munro and his father near Poplar and Lauderdale. Diggs parked, jumped out and walked up to Munro with a .45-caliber Smith and Wesson revolver. Diggs shot Munro in the leg, turned and walked back toward his car without saying anything. The bullet shattered the bone in Munro's left leg between the knee and hip.[208]

Officers Jack Sherrill and Patrick Roberts heard the shot from the rear of the pharmacy, ran out and disarmed Diggs. Once they put handcuffs on him, Munro's father attacked Diggs, causing severe lacerations to his head and face. The officers had to beat Sanders so badly with nightsticks to get him off Diggs that an ambulance had to carry him to St. Joseph's Hospital. The officers charged Diggs with shooting with intent to kill and carrying a pistol, but he was out of jail within an hour on a bond signed by Dr. E.A. Gillespie and his sister-in-law.[209]

Diggs missed his November court date, so his counsel, Shelby County attorney Tyler McClain, gave Judge Harsh a medical excuse written by Dr. Bramlett of Clarksdale, Mississippi. Unsatisfied by the letter, Harsh revoked Diggs's bonds and ordered him to appear in court. The judge, however, had to delay the trial again while Diggs recovered from an illness and Monro recovered from another leg injury. After more delays because of Diggs's other sentencings, Munro eventually dropped the charges and surprised his doctors and fans when he made a comeback in 1925.[210]

In October 1922, Diggs outraged residents of Clarksdale, Mississippi, when he announced his plans to open a pharmacy in their town. A few weeks later, members of the chamber of commerce, Rotary Club, Kiwanis Club, Lions' Club, Clarksdale Associated Retailers, Woman's Club, League of Women Voters and Mothers' Club passed a resolution to inform Diggs that his presence was "undesirable" and he should vacate the county. Mayor Ellington Fant then instructed the city clerk not to issue Diggs a license for his store. Asked if he worried about a legal challenge, Fant stated, "I don't think [Diggs] can get a lawyer in this community to handle the case."[211]

Leaving Shelby County had been a violation of Diggs's bond. Sheriff's deputies arrested him when he returned from Clarksdale, and Judge Harsh doubled Diggs's bond at the request of Shelby County attorney general Sam O. Bates. Diggs's attorney, Charles M. Bryan, filed a motion for a new trial and promised to appeal to the Supreme Court if that did not work.[212]

Diggs had destroyed his reputation by sheltering his outlaw friends and paying thousands of dollars of their legal fees. Now he sat friendless in the Shelby County Jail with no one to return the favor. His last hope had been the Wilkerson brothers. He assumed that because of their long history of selling legal and illegal drugs, the Wilkersons would try to keep Diggs out of jail, but they reneged on their promise to pay his bond. Diggs, in no condition to stay in jail, fumed over their betrayal and planned his revenge against them.[213]

Diggs began suffering from morphine withdrawal after jailer James G. Chambers clamped down on drug trafficking in the jail. Visitors would secretly give drugs to inmates through handshakes. "Then too, when [prisoners] are first sent in," explained Chambers, "they have the ability to secret enough drugs to do for several weeks in places on their person that are unmentionable."[214]

Dr. E.E. Lunsford tried to help Diggs as much as possible. Lunsford, arrested for narcotics violations, had gone through withdrawal three months earlier. The intense abdominal pains, nausea, vomiting, diarrhea, anxiety and insomnia kept Diggs bedridden. "Diggs wants to get off the habit," said Lunsford. "Only his intense desire to get rid of it holds him up as well as it does."[215]

As Diggs suffered through withdrawal, he heard the news that someone had killed Frank Holloway. Diggs told reporters from his cell that he knew who gunned down his mentor but refused to name the vengeful killer. The reporter asked Diggs what he thought of the story that Holloway said he was going straight. "Straight?" exclaimed Diggs. "It wasn't in him."[216]

Police found Holloway's bullet-scarred body in a shallow grave on Pistol Hill near Tulsa, Oklahoma. Diggs believed Holloway had confided in a woman who betrayed him to his pursuers. His larger-than-life hero was bound, gagged and shot in the head twice before being jammed into a hole by the former associates he betrayed.[217]

Diggs had been out on bond less than a month when police found him with an African American man named Henry Green in Diggs's car parked in front of 353 South Fourth Street negotiating the purchase of six one-eighth-ounce bottles of morphine. His March 29 arrest was the last news Ella Nolen heard about her son. Her Ella Nolen's condition had taken a turn for the worse, so she had returned to Memphis to spend her final days with

Ernest Nolen and her grandchildren. She died from respiratory problems two days later as Diggs Nolen's attorney negotiated his bond.[218]

Following the funeral, Diggs squabbled with Ernest over their mother's furniture and collection of cut glass. Diggs purchased the items for his mother, but she willed them to Ernest. After she died, Ernest put them in storage and refused to return them to his brother. Their first court date ended without a decision because the brothers got in a fistfight. Their lawyers wanted another court date as soon as possible before Diggs began his sentence for forgery; however, Diggs landed in more trouble before they could settle the matter.[219]

In June 1923, Diggs tried another phony check scheme to pay for his increasingly expensive drug habit. Diggs asked attorney Ernest Bell to vouch for twenty-one-year-old W.R. Caine, a.k.a. R.L. Watson, who had a $5,000 check to cash. He offered Bell $500 in exchange for his help as a way to repay him for representing him the previous Friday in court. Bell and Caine went to the Security Bank and Trust at 84 Madison Avenue, where Bell introduced Caine to bank president Theodore Read. Assuming the check was good, Bell suggested that the banker call Citizens' Bank of Winona, Mississippi, to verify its authenticity.

Diggs became anxious while waiting outside. While Read waited for a reply from Winona, Diggs stormed in and said he had "no time for this foolishness." He grabbed the check and walked outside. Bell followed him, and the two argued on the street briefly before Bell talked Diggs into going back to the bank to wait for the reply. They came back in to find that the banker in Winona had called back and told Read the check was fake.[220]

Police sergeant Tom Couch and Patrolman Albert Rogers noticed Diggs leave the bank in a hurry with Caine and Bell. The officers had recently arrested Caine for vagrancy and became suspicious when they saw the young man with Diggs. They approached the three, and Diggs fled on foot. Bell, angry about being duped, explained what happened and asked the officers to track down and arrest Diggs. On Bell's tip, they found Diggs and his wife registered as Mr. and Mrs. James Harris at the Fransioli Hotel, where they took him into custody.[221]

Bell was cleared of any wrongdoing but felt humiliated. Caine, described by his lawyer as a simple country boy, claimed that Diggs had put him under a "hypnotic spell." Bell, however, had no excuses. Judge Fitzhugh scolded Bell, saying his client's reputation as an "arch-criminal" should have put him on notice. He told Bell that any lawyer, knowing Diggs's reputation, "ought to be careful about having any sort of transactions with him when it involved any sort of paper like a check, or anything of that sort."[222]

On June 15, Diggs was found guilty on two charges of violating the Harrison Anti-Narcotic Act stemming from his arrest on March 29. Judge Ross asked federal district attorney Eugene Murray to dispose of the three other indictments against Nolen as quickly as possible. On June 22, Diggs pleaded guilty to two counts of violating the Harrison Anti-Narcotic Act. He received a five-year sentence in the Atlanta federal prison and a $1,000 fine.[223]

"He's a helpless addict," explained Charles M. Bryan as he entered Diggs's guilty plea. Bryan told Judge J.W. Ross that his client had been a drug addict for the last two years and he hoped incarceration would help cure his drug habit. Those who knew Diggs agreed that a prison sentence was a blessing in disguise. They felt that the routine of prison life, regular habits, medical treatment, regular meals and exercise would restore Diggs to health and vigor.[224]

As he prepared for prison, Diggs once again became a topic in a mayoral election. The 1923 election was a three-way battle between the current mayor, Rowlett Paine; Judge Lewis Fitzhugh; and Ku Klux Klan candidate Joe Wood. Paine once again seized the opportunity to tie Diggs to a political opponent. Because Diggs had helped the police in some investigations, Fitzhugh had shown him some sympathy in court and in the press. Paine tried to frame Fitzhugh's remarks about Diggs as evidence of collusion with the underworld.[225]

Charles M. Bryan acted as the de facto campaign manager for Fitzhugh. Paine used Bryan's association with Diggs as further evidence of Fitzhugh's ties to Diggs. Paine stalwart Commissioner Tom Allen began his attack by saying, "Every time I see the name Charles Bryan in print, I smell the odor of Diggs Nolen and stolen bonds."[226]

Diggs's downward emotional spiral kept him from commenting on or even caring about the election. His ruined reputation because of O'Reilly's charges had made it impossible for him to conduct legitimate business. Even worse, two of the most important people in his life, his mother and Frank Holloway, had recently died. The shock of the two deaths and the physical pain he still suffered from his gunshot wounds, alcoholism and addiction wore heavily on him.

Diggs's crimes became less about personal gain than supporting his drug habit and railing against authority. Diggs had married the nurse who tended him after Ethel shot him, but even her love was not enough to make him change his ways. His friends and family believed that incarceration was the only way to save him from self-destruction. However, Diggs did not see it that way; he had no desire to return to prison. If his lawyers could not get him out of jail, he would find a way out himself.[227]

Chapter 16

ESCAPE

Diggs Nolen has gone away. He passed away like a midsummer's dream.
He vanished in thin air like the ghost of Hamlet's father.[228]
—*Malcom Patterson*

The judges in Diggs Nolen's different cases had to figure out which sentence he would serve first. Even though Diggs was already in the Atlanta federal prison, they agreed in July 1923 to have him serve his three- to fifteen-year term for forgery in Nashville before serving his five-year term in Atlanta for narcotics violations. They kept their gentlemen's agreement secret because they needed Diggs's testimony in the case against the Wilkerson brothers and they did not want to anger him and risk losing his cooperation. They agreed that once Diggs came back to Memphis to testify, state authorities would take custody of him and transfer him to Nashville.[229]

Diggs found out about the deal from his lawyer when marshals transferred him from the Atlanta penitentiary for the trial in December 1923. He pleaded with U.S. district attorney Eugene Murray to send him back to Atlanta, but Murray refused to help. Diggs, furious about his impending transfer, made plans to escape. He became friendly and cooperative to get his handlers to lower their guards. Before long, his jailers were allowing Diggs to receive money and whiskey from visitors. They also allowed him to wear nice suits; visit his pharmacy, now run by Ernest; and visit his wife at her exclusive hotel, paid for by the U.S. Justice Department.[230]

Diggs told friends that he intended to implicate Lynn and Warren Wilkerson in the dope ring because they had "left him to rot in jail." News of Diggs's impending testimony sent those involved into hiding. Diggs, eager to appear cooperative, volunteered to help U.S. deputy marshal Newt Butler and federal narcotics agent F.A. Feimster search for missing witnesses.[231]

Diggs talked Butler into letting him go to Jansen's Restaurant and a show at the Pantages Theater with his wife during a break in the search. The deputy marshal agreed and accompanied the two to the theater. During the show, Diggs excused himself to go to the restroom. The show and conversation with Margaret kept Butler distracted long enough for Diggs to sneak out a back door.[232]

Diggs Nolen, Memphis Police Department mug shot, circa 1920. *Courtesy of Memphis Public Library and Information Center.*

Diggs's escape became a sensation across the South. Reporters said Diggs's "dare-devil escape" had made a "laughing stock" of local law enforcement. Some even suggested Diggs had bribed his way to freedom. Police, deputies, marshals and even Boy Scouts scoured the city and surrounding areas chasing down tips about Diggs's whereabouts. Police raided the home of bootlegger James Mulcahy, where they found fourteen five-gallon cans of corn liquor but no Diggs. Someone claimed to have seen Diggs in Moscow, Tennessee, where he pawned his overcoat to pay for a train ticket to Iuka, Mississippi. Rumors of Diggs's escapades ranged from crossing Hudson Bay into Canada to taking up with Mexican bandits.[233]

Diggs's escape was not so elaborate. The man described as the "wily rogue and mastermind of the underworld" had simply slipped out of the theater, caught a taxi and had the driver drop him off on the outskirts of the city. Diggs walked to Hornlake, Mississippi, and slept in a railroad station. He borrowed some money from a friend and took a train to Sardis, Mississippi, the following morning. Then he took another train to New Orleans, where he hoped no one would recognize him.[234]

On December 10, Detective Jacobs of the New Orleans Police Department spotted a familiar face while on patrol on Canal Street with his partner, Detective Dominguez. Jacobs stopped and asked the stranger his name. He said his name was Applegate and he worked at the Jefferson Park horse track. Jacobs recognized him as soon as he spoke. It was Diggs Nolen.[235]

Jacobs grabbed Diggs and took him into custody. Jacobs told him, "I'll never forget you. I arrested you eight years ago at the Louisville and Nashville Station when you tried to shoot me!" Tulane had recently expelled Diggs because of a prank, and he got into trouble at the train station. Diggs shot at Jacobs when he tried to make the arrest. Fortunately for the detective, Diggs's pistol misfired.[236]

Federal district judge Rufus Foster signed the order for Diggs's removal on December 13, and Chief Deputy Marshal Charles Sullivan transported him back to Memphis. Local marshals returned Diggs to the custody of the Tennessee State Penitentiary on December 21, 1923. Diggs was unhappy about the transfer, but that did not stop him from making friends among the guards again. Before long, they took him off manual labor duties and assigned him to deliver mail and run errands for them. All the while, Diggs kept watch for the next opportunity to escape.[237]

IN MEMPHIS, U.S. DISTRICT attorney Eugene Murray had been looking to convict Lynn and Warren Wilkerson for illegally trafficking narcotics. In September 1922, George Draper, chief of the Federal Narcotics Division in Tennessee, assigned agent Cecil Frazier to investigate the brothers' wholesale drug company. Frazier, who had led successful investigations in the Southwest, quickly picked up the trail of a young pharmacist and illegal narcotics courier named Van A. Spring.

Frazier and Agent E.A. Feinster tried to arrest Spring near Front and Vance as he left Wilkerson Brothers with two packages of heroin and cocaine. Spring bolted, and Frazier shot him as he ran away. The agents carried the wounded Spring into the Wilkerson store and called for an ambulance. Spring whispered to Frazier, "I've got something to tell you, but I dare not tell you in this store." Spring later died at St. Joseph's Hospital before he could reveal his secret, but Murray suspected that the Wilkersons were only parts of a much bigger narcotics ring and Diggs Nolen was the key to uncovering it.[238]

Murray knew that Diggs and the Wilkersons were on bad terms and expected Diggs to provide damning testimony against his former supplier. Diggs, however, had become increasingly mercurial since he found out that the DA planned to send him to the state prison after the trial. The days dragged on in the crowded cellblock in the sweltering heat. Diggs, anxious and bored, decided he'd had enough.[239]

Daylight peeked through the crack, and fresh air cooled the sweat on Diggs Nolen's face. He and the others in the tunnel picked up their pace. The prisoners in the cell sang to drown out the sound of the crumbling wall.

And now we are aged and gray, Maggie, and the trials of life nearly done!

The jailer would be back soon to make his rounds. They dug faster. Equipped with nothing more than a fork, a knife, a can opener and two pieces of an iron bed, they pried the old mortar loose. The singers raised their voices to match the feverish chiseling.

Let us sing of the days that are gone, Maggie, when you and I were young!

Diggs punched through the two-foot wall and shimmied out. One by one, the others squeezed past the jagged pieces of brick and dropped to the ground. S.H. Moore got stuck. It took pushing from one end and pulling from the other to get him through. Cut and bruised, Moore cleared the wall and ran for freedom. A man walking by the jail saw the prisoners and ran to the front gate to warn the guards. Forty prisoners passed through the narrow opening before jailer James G. Chambers, and the other deputies made it to the cellblock.[240]

Twenty-two-year-old Leonard Coleman slammed on the breaks of his Union Company Clothing truck to keep from hitting an escapee. The young African American man watched as fifteen convicts ran across Second Street and disappeared into alleys and side streets. Before he could put his truck back into gear, his door swung open and he felt a knife against his ribs. Diggs and bank robber Ben Adams climbed into the cab and ordered Coleman to drive. He drove several blocks to Decatur and Jackson Avenue, where the escapees forced him out and stole the truck.[241]

"That dope fellow made us all like him. He sure had brains," said car thief Louis McAlexander. "He bought us coca-colas and cigarettes and things. He called us all together Monday afternoon after lunch and told us how we could get out. We started to work. He did most of it. He sure did know how to go about it too."[242]

Diggs Nolen, after several days of stirring discontent, convinced his fellow prisoners to break out of jail on Monday, June 23, 1924. Those not digging sang "When You and I Were Young, Maggie" and "Sweet Adeline"

Louis McAlexander, Memphis Police Department mug shot, 1924. *Courtesy of Memphis Public Library and Information Center.*

to distract the guards. By five o'clock in the afternoon, Diggs had tunneled through the two-foot-thick wall and led the biggest jailbreak in the history of Memphis and Shelby County.[243]

Margaret May Nolen pleaded with her husband to turn himself in. She promised to wait for him, no matter how long he remained behind bars. Diggs relented, but he was in no hurry to surrender to police. With nowhere to go, he rode around in the back of a taxi and drank whiskey until he passed out. The driver returned to the taxi stand at Linden and Mulberry Street at about two forty-five and called Deputy Sheriff Charles Garibaldi. Deputies Edgar Harris and Stratton Barbaro arrived and found Diggs "blind drunk" in the cab, so they had the driver deliver him to the jail.

As the deputies carried Diggs out of the taxi, he regained consciousness and began to fight. The deputies subdued Diggs and put him in the so-called condemned cell. This cell was nothing more than an eight-foot-long container with sheet metal sides and roof. It had some holes for air and a slot to pass food through and contained only a bunk and small lavatory.[244]

"For a day, we were regaled with stories of how Diggs Nolen was the mastermind of the great escape," an editorial writer commented. "We expected Diggs to make a brave fight with guns and bombs if he was detected, but the next day Diggs was found, minus his shirt, and some say his pants, snoozing in a taxicab. He surrendered ingloriously. He opined that he merely wanted to get out to get a little liquor."[245]

Sheriff Will Knight suspended jailer James G. Chambers and day guard Sam Walker. Chambers blamed Diggs for the jailbreak. "Diggs was a troublemaker from the time that he was brought here," he stated. "From him the spirit of unrest spread to the rest of the prisoners." According to Chambers, Diggs sowed discontent by claiming the jailers overcharged for sodas.[246]

Diggs, painfully hungover, admitted to a reporter that he spread the story about the sodas but denied having masterminded the escape. "The way of the transgressor is hard," he quoted humorist Kin Hubbard with a sigh. "I suppose that is right. That is the way of transgressors who get caught."[247]

"Vanity, yea, all is vanity," he quoted Ecclesiastes. "The old prophet was right. Goodness knows that I am not all bad. I am human and have had my dreams with the rest." He pontificated on the subjects of morality and the futility of human endeavor until he started to feel the ill effects of the moonshine again. "I feel all snaky," he groaned as he concluded the interview.[248]

Diggs also felt mistreated by the U.S. district attorney. Diggs had appeared in Eugene Murray's office partially clothed and demanded a new suit. Murray refused. Then Margaret drove in from Ohio and asked to be a witness for the prosecution. Murray would have had to pay her ten cents per mile traveled to Memphis had he agreed. The DA again refused.[249]

Diggs complained, "They [the DA's office] had shown me no consideration. Why should I testify? If I thought they didn't want me to, I would. But I believe they want me to, so I won't." Diggs, as he promised, took the stand but refused to cooperate.[250]

"I don't want to testify in this case!"

"What objections have you?" asked Murray.

"Anything I would say might incriminate myself." Turning to the jury, Diggs added, "The district attorney's attitude towards me has something to do with my decision."[251]

Attorney D.B. Puryear asked Judge John Ross to remind Diggs of his rights in giving testimony that might be used as evidence against him. Ross told Diggs that any testimony would not be used against him, but he could not change his mind. "I'm not going to testify," declared Diggs. He argued with the DA until Ross reprimanded him. Murray gave up and asked the judge to excuse Diggs. The DA then ordered Diggs sent to the Tennessee State Penitentiary to begin his sentence for forgery.[252]

Diggs set in motion the derailment of Murray's case against the Wilkerson brothers. Witness William Billers followed Diggs's example and refused to testify as well. Murray's case fell apart. The judge freed the Wilkersons after they pleaded no contest and paid a $10,000 fine.[253]

In March 1925, Diggs asked Warden A.A. McCorkle to go to Nashville to see a dentist. McCorkle assigned a guard to take Diggs to the city. Along the way, Diggs convinced the guard to take a detour. Diggs snuck away, called a cab and forced the driver to take him to Hopkinsville, Kentucky. Sam Harper, another guard, tracked down Diggs and returned him to prison. Diggs, now a third-grade prisoner, wore a special striped uniform, could neither write nor receive letters and lost entertainment privileges, including movies and baseball games.[254]

Every escape attempt, in the end, had only ensured a longer prison sentence. Diggs's prospects seemed gloomy until he got an encouraging message from his legal team. Despite every obstacle he faced and every obstacle he'd created, his lawyers found a loophole. It was a long shot, but it was enough to give him hope that he might win his freedom at last.

Chapter 17
PAROLE

Diggs Nolen is the embodiment of lawlessness.
—Mayor Rowlett Paine, June 1926

S he'll be waiting," Diggs Nolen insisted, "no matter when I get out. And we're going away and start all over again." Sitting in the cell with Diggs, Tom Little took notes and made sketches. The reporter and cartoonist had a soft spot for the downtrodden and those down on their luck. He knew that Margaret had left Diggs, but he let him talk anyway. "And pal, while you're writing about me, won't you just forget her name?" Diggs said she had inspired him to give up his old ways for the "new and righteous" life he intended to lead after his release.[255]

Diggs's bid for freedom would not be easy. His lawyers faced complicated legal challenges because of his overlapping federal and state sentences. They also had to find a way around Diggs's voluntary exile agreement. However, their biggest hurdle was Rowlett Paine's opposition to Diggs's parole. Paine despised Diggs, and the Memphis mayor would do almost anything to keep the outlaw from returning to his city.

In June 1926, Tennessee prison authorities planned to parole Diggs and turn him over to federal authorities to serve the remainder of his sentence from his narcotics trial. Charles M. Bryan argued that Nolen's federal sentence ended when Atlanta Federal Penitentiary officials turned Diggs over to the Tennessee State Prison. He insisted that the suspension of Diggs's federal sentence until his state sentence ended was illegal.[256]

Diggs Nolen, 1927. *Courtesy of Memphis Public Library and Information Center.*

Bryan based his argument on a recent case involving Dr. Frederick Albert Cook. The famed explorer who claimed to have reached the North Pole a year before Robert Peary started a shady oil business in Texas. A jury convicted him of fraud. During the appeal hearings, the judge ruled that once a federal sentence has begun, it cannot be suspended.[257]

Diggs promised to lead a law-abiding life if given a chance. "I have broken the law a number of times in the past," he told reporter W.P. Kerrigan Jr., "and believe me, when you get in trouble it's no easy matter to get out. But if they will let me alone when I get out of this, I'll go to some city and go absolutely straight." He planned to sell his remaining property in Memphis to take his case to the Tennessee Supreme Court, if necessary.[258]

Diggs even passed up a chance to escape. In April 1926, seventeen prisoners slipped through a window of the state prison, including William Annadale, who broke out of the Shelby County Jail with Diggs in June 1924. Diggs watched but did not participate. The veteran of numerous jailbreaks, now older and somewhat wiser, knew his best chance at freedom lay with his lawyers. Diggs would reach his minimum sentence required for consideration in June 1927, and he did not want to spoil his chances of release. The parole board also acknowledged the weakness of the case that led to Diggs's conviction and that his prior criminal record played a part in his sentencing.[259]

The Memphis mayor sent a telegram followed by a letter in protest to Governor Austin Peay insisting Diggs serve his full sentence in the interest of law enforcement. Paine called Diggs's mere presence a menace to the peace and safety of the people. He claimed that Diggs led a notorious criminal ring that had terrorized and demoralized the city for years. He said the "dope problem" in Memphis had practically been solved since Diggs's incarceration. Paine included Diggs's criminal record to convince Peay not to turn him loose on Memphis again.[260]

The timing could not have been worse for the mayor. Paine had his hands full dealing with the aftermath of the 1927 Mississippi Valley flood and the police department bribery scandal involving the John Belluomini payoff books. He needed to keep the pressure on Peay, so he called on the

Governor Austin Peay. *Courtesy of Memphis Public Library and Information Center.*

local chapter of the Lions Club and other civic organizations to send the governor letters and telegrams denouncing any thought of paroling Diggs.[261]

The governor sympathized with Paine, but he felt that Diggs had served an adequate sentence. Peay signed the parole but included conditions he thought would appease the Memphis mayor. Peay acted on an 1843 Tennessee statute that stated the governor may grant pardons with such restrictions and limitations as he may deem proper. Diggs's conditional parole would stay in effect as long as he "does not violate the law and lives the life of a good citizen, and he does not return to the city of Memphis." The document further stated that "if he violates either of these conditions, he may be returned to the prison to serve the remainder of his sentence."[262]

Diggs found U.S. marshals waiting for him when he walked out of the Tennessee State Prison on July 8, 1927. To Diggs's surprise, they took him to Leavenworth rather than the Atlanta Federal Penitentiary. The Atlanta warden had requested that Diggs go to Leavenworth because he did not want the headache of dealing with another celebrity outlaw like the "Count of Gramercy Park," Gerald Chapman. Guards kept their travel plans secret so that Diggs's cohorts could not free him during the trip.[263]

Charles Bryan telegrammed Diggs, "Worked to death fighting Paine." In October 1927, Bryan filed a writ of habeas corpus, arguing that because Diggs had served his federal and state sentences simultaneously, he should be freed. Bryan also argued that Judge Ross had no right to suspend Diggs's sentence without him present.[264]

Federal judge John C. Pollock of Kansas City agreed with Bryan's argument and ruled that Diggs's federal term had expired. Pollock also upheld the contention that Judge Ross could not act in a felony case without the defendant's presence. Diggs was free again but still exiled from Tennessee.[265]

On October 31, 1927, Bryan received a telegram from Diggs. "Judge Pollock released me," he wrote. "Your contention sustained. Notify Roving Rowlett." Bryan delivered the message and infuriated the mayor. In a bitter mayoral campaign against Ed Crump stalwart Watkins Overton, Paine accused the Crump political machine of helping Diggs. He claimed Bryan, another Crump supporter, had secured Diggs's freedom in retribution for Paine's efforts to bring to justice John Belluomini, a bootlegger he falsely accused of working for Crump.[266]

Diggs left for Florida to work for William Huntley, his coconspirator from the Liberty bonds heist. He was in Miami for only eight hours before police raided the house where he was staying and threw everyone out. They put him on a train for Tampa, but police there ran him out of town as soon as he arrived. The same scenario played out wherever he went. With nowhere else to go, Diggs snuck back into Memphis on November 13, 1927.

Three days later, police detectives received word that Diggs Nolen had returned to the city. Detectives Mario Chiozza, Lee Quianthy and William Rainer arrived at Ernest Nolen's drugstore at four o'clock in the afternoon and found Diggs working in the back. Chiozza said, "Diggs, we want you." Diggs, without a word, picked up his hat and coat and left with the detectives.[267]

"I am a man without a country! They have kicked me from pillar to post." Diggs asked the desk sergeant with a dramatic flourish, "What must I do?" Lawyer Ralph Davis filed a habeas corpus writ for Diggs's release. Davis contended that the parole board had overstepped its authority by forcing Diggs to agree to exile. Judge Ben Capell issued a continuance and released Diggs on a $500 bond.[268]

Diggs returned to court and sat with his chin in his hand, listening intently to the arguments. Once on the stand, he described how he was "hounded from place to place" by local police and eventually forced to come back to Memphis. Diggs's case presented the first time anyone resisted the terms of a conditional pardon in Tennessee. Lawyers flocked to the courtroom to hear the case argued. With no Tennessee example to go by, they wondered what procedure the court would use to determine Diggs's fate.[269]

"The pardon that was issued on July 8 says specifically that [Diggs] Nolen may not return to the city of Memphis," Davis told the court. "It also says that he shall be delivered to the warden of the government penitentiary of Fort Leavenworth, Kansas. This pardon was merely given Nolen so that he could leave the state prison and become a government prisoner and the stipulation as to his return to Memphis is couched in language of the present tense and not applicable to a date after he had served out his federal sentence."

The court members, so focused on the stormy proceedings, did not notice that Diggs Nolen had slipped out of the courthouse until the session concluded. Police and deputies combed the city once they realized what Diggs had done. They thought he had left Memphis until Ernest Nolen called late in the evening to let them know his brother was at his house. He promised to return Diggs the following morning, so Judge Capell told the deputies to leave Diggs in his care. The court gathered, expecting Diggs not to show up. At 9:55 a.m., Diggs sauntered back into the courtroom as if nothing had happened. Police and deputies breathed a sigh of relief and put it down to "just one of Diggs's pranks." Capell granted Davis's motion for a new habeas corpus hearing and released Diggs until the next court date.[270]

Diggs Nolen's supporters, including Judge Malcom Patterson, gathered petitions to give to Governor Henry Horton during his visit to the city on his inspection of state highways. "I believe [Diggs] Nolen has been shamefully treated," said Patterson. "Nolen should be given his liberty and not returned to Nashville as I believe his is a badly abused man and has amply paid for whatever sins he may have committed." Horton, however, would not consider the case until Davis exhausted all legal avenues and Diggs Nolen surrendered to prison authorities.[271]

Capell felt Diggs had served an adequate sentence but felt compelled to uphold the terms of his pardon. On December 15, 1927, he ruled that Diggs violated the conditions of his parole and ordered him returned to the state prison to serve the remainder of his fifteen-year sentence for forgery. Davis appealed the decision, asked for a new trial and prepared an appeal to the state supreme court. In the meantime, Diggs was free to roam Memphis while he waited for a new trial.[272]

Chapter 18
THE THIRD SALLY

Diggs Nolen isn't crazy; he just wants an honest job.
—The Commercial Appeal, *August 1928*

Diggs Nolen wondered if he was crazy. He sat in his cell and thought about what the doctor had said about him. He'd always felt a need to pursue the outlaw life, even at the expense of his well-being and relationships with those he loved. He had faced many judges, juries, newspaper reporters and parole boards. Each time, he claimed to be rehabilitated and promised to lead a law-abiding life going forward. Each time, he forgot his promises as soon as he was set free. Each time through the cycle, he came out worse off than before. Now he had hit rock bottom.

The jailer came to escort Diggs to see the doctor again. He would once more promise to turn his life around. It might work, and he might even mean it, but he would first have to convince the judge, the doctors and his family he was sane. That might not be so easy, considering how he had been living the last eight months.

Diggs, free while waiting for his appeal, had found himself in another kind of prison. His wife had left him, and his adventures had come to an end. He no longer had a legitimate business to run nor illegal outlets for income. The notoriety he once craved had deprived him of any opportunity to lead a normal, productive life. He could not even leave the city to start somewhere new without risk of further arrests. Instead, he spent his time getting in trouble for no other reasons than boredom and an urge to lash out at authority.

The year 1928 began with a long series of arrests for drunk, disorderly and suspicious conduct. Diggs celebrated the new year with highway robber Tommy Layman, an associate of fellow Shelby County Jail escapee William Annadale. The two celebrated at an apartment at Lauderdale Street and Washington Avenue. Lieutenant Granville Heckle and Detective Sergeants W.J. Rainey and Lee Quianthy arrested the two after neighbors complained of the noise.[273]

Ten days later, Ernest Nolen received a call at his pharmacy that Ethel Wikoff's new husband, Maurice Pian, had pulled a pistol on Diggs. Ernest took a cab and rushed to a nightclub run by bootlegger Andy Wallace at 617 Monroe Avenue. He found his brother and Pian squared off for a fight. Ernest grabbed Diggs, forced him into the cab and took him to the police station. Ernest had the police hold Diggs in a cell until he sobered up and calmed down. Officers went to the nightclub, but Pian left before they could arrest him.[274]

In March 1928, Diggs's old friend Hart Austin returned to Memphis. Austin had garnered a reputation as a bank robber and murderer in the United States and Canada since Griffin ran him out of the city in 1920. In December 1924, Austin returned to rob a bank with local police characters Jack Dillon and Henry Laughter. Mrs. J.W. Buchan, his nosy landlady, overheard their plans to rob the South Side Bank and tipped off the police. Before they arrived, she forced Austin to surrender with a shotgun. He was extradited to Canada to serve a term for robbery, and Mrs. Buchan received a $500 reward from the Canadian government.[275]

After his release, Austin reached out to his old friends Diggs Nolen and Neils Keren "Popeye" Pumphrey. Popeye was educated and came from a well-to-do family. He took part in bank robberies, high-stakes gambling scams and other antics. Like Diggs, he sought out daring crimes, and much to the chagrin of law enforcement, he avoided any serious jail time. The gathering of the three notable outlaws raised concerns among law enforcement. Griffin arrested them after receiving a tip that the trio was planning a bank robbery. The detective released Diggs and Popeye with a warning not to pull any capers.[276]

Austin did not get off so easy. Griffin wanted the vicious gunman out of Memphis for good. "This town is not big enough for the both of us, and I'm not leaving," Griffin told Austin. The inspector and three other officers threw Austin into a patrol car and drove him to Arkansas. They pulled over to the side of the road near Marion. According to Griffin, they "pitched him out in a mudhole and told him to keep going."[277]

William T. Griffin, inspector of detectives, 1924. *Courtesy of Memphis Public Library and Information Center.*

Griffin and Lieutenant Lee Quianthy arrested Diggs again two days later hanging around another pair of out-of-town hoodlums, John Hull of Chicago and H.B. Myers of St. Louis. "Well boys," Diggs told the officers at the police headquarters, "here I am again!" Griffin released Diggs since he did not have enough evidence to hold him but gave him another stern warning before letting him go.[278]

The talking-to seemed to deter Diggs from planning any more robberies, but it did little good in getting him to stop drinking. On June 2, 1928, Sergeant Julio Vannucci and Patrolman W.W. Herrington responded to another complaint after Diggs got drunk and beat up his landlady, Mrs. Joe Manley, at her home at 346 Washington Avenue. Two weeks later, the Shelby County Grand Jury indicted him once again for carrying a pistol.[279]

When he wasn't being arrested, Diggs drank illegal moonshine incessantly and wandered about downtown Memphis. One day in August, he was so drunk that he stumbled over a crack in the sidewalk, fell and struck his head on the pavement. He continued on his bender until Ernest became so worried about his brother that he swore out an insanity warrant and had him arrested.[280]

Holloway had captivated Ernest with his stories and inspired him to take up the outlaw life; however, unlike Diggs, Ernest knew when to give it up. Ernest served a seventeen-month sentence in Leavenworth Prison for attempting to free Diggs. After his pardon from President Wilson, he landed a job as undersheriff of Ottawa County, Kansas. He held the position until political rivals circulated his prison record during the next election. Ernest returned to Memphis, where he and his wife, Margaret, started a family and worked in their pharmacy.[281]

Diggs, however, kept Ernest's life from being anything but ordinary. Ernest helped Diggs get surgery in April to finally remove the bullet from Ethel's pistol lodged in his abdomen. A month later, Diggs and Ernest visited their father's store in Telly Switch, Mississippi. While the brothers were standing on the porch, two ex-convicts tried to gun them down. The bullets missed Diggs, but one struck Ernest in the leg. Diggs rushed Ernest to St. Joseph's Hospital in Memphis for emergency surgery.[282]

Memphis Police Department headquarters, circa 1924. *Courtesy of Memphis Public Library and Information Center.*

The burden of caring for his self-destructing brother wore heavily on Ernest. Diggs eventually reached a point where Ernest thought his brother was completely out-of-control. Ernest, desperate for help, reached out to the police. Police physician Dr. Neumon Taylor examined Diggs and recommended for the "benefit of his welfare that he spend some time in some secluded insane asylum." Guards locked Diggs up until his appearance before a judge the following day.[283]

Diggs spent the night coming to terms with where his life had taken him. People no longer saw him as a criminal mastermind but rather a drunken lunatic. Perhaps, as the fog of alcohol and drugs began to fade, he began to see that his problem was not the prison where he sat but the prison he had created for himself. He had ruined his business and alienated friends and loved ones to imitate a desperado who died face down in a ditch with two bullets in his head. With his reason free and clear, maybe he saw through the deceptions and absurdities of the outlaw life.

Diggs came to his senses the following morning, because of either an epiphany or the prospect of being institutionalized. He also found help from an unlikely friend. A lucid and penitent Diggs appeared before Squire E.E. Jeter with the surprising announcement that he had a job. Inspector Will Griffin, who had arrested Diggs many times, had taken pity on him and called in some favors. After many refusals, Griffin landed Diggs a position at the local automotive plant.

Diggs, in high spirits despite a terrible headache, playfully addressed the charges. Jail physician Dr. T.C. Graves examined Nolen and announced, "No, I don't think Diggs is crazy."

Diggs replied, "Of course I'm not crazy. You're crazy if you think I'm crazy."

"Well, I don't think you're crazy."

"Then, that shows you're not crazy. I wonder who is crazy now!"

Diggs's father, James Nolen, confirmed his son's story to the judge. "Yes, it's a fact. Inspector Griffin got him a job at the Fisher Body Plant, and he starts Wednesday"—he glared at his son—"if he don't get drunk."

"Oh, I'm through drinking," promised Diggs. "I really mean it. I've got a job now after walking the street for days and days." Diggs told the judge that he had applied for many jobs, but no one would hire him because of his reputation. "It was tough sailing, I tell you," said Diggs. "But now I've got a chance and I'm going to make good."

Jeter considered Diggs's plea. On the one hand, Jeter had the chance to keep the troublesome police character off the streets for a while. On

Courtroom, Shelby County Courthouse. *Courtesy of Memphis Public Library and Information Center.*

the other hand, the Nolens appeared sincere in their desire to save Diggs. Inspector Griffin had gone through a lot of trouble to find him a job, and James and Ernest appeared willing to supervise Diggs during his recovery. The elder Nolen promised he would "whip him like he was an imp of a boy" if Diggs did not behave. Ernest assured Jeter that he would help make sure it was done right.[284]

Jeter, satisfied with the Nolens' promises, decided to give Diggs another chance. He ruled that Diggs was sane and ordered him released. Jeter worried Diggs's notoriety might cause undue attention, so he suggested that Diggs use another name until he proved he could hold a job to the satisfaction of his new boss. Diggs agreed. The gavel tapped, and Diggs was free again.[285]

Chapter 19

HOME

I will never leave Memphis. Somehow, I feel I never will
because I've got no home but Memphis.
—Diggs Nolen, August 1928

James Nolen had to sit down and catch his breath. Ernest, Maggie and their children sat down to join him for supper, but James did not feel like eating. He had not had much of an appetite recently, and he felt fatigued today. The excitement of the day seemed to have caught up with him. He hoped some rest might soothe his sore muscles.

Earlier that day, James, Ernest and Diggs left the courthouse victorious. They felt a renewed sense of hope as they walked under the hot August sun. Diggs was sober and eager to start his new job. James and Ernest were hopeful that Diggs was finally leaving the outlaw life behind. It was a happy moment for the Nolens.

The house rumbled from a thunderstorm. James woke and saw rain pelting the windows as he struggled to sit up in bed. His body ached all over, and his mind seemed to be in a fog. He rolled out of bed, stood up and took a few steps. The fog turned to darkness. Ernest found his father unconscious on the floor and rushed him to St. Joseph's Hospital, where doctors determined he was suffering from uremic poisoning. James slipped into a coma as his kidneys began to fail.[286]

Diggs never made it to work on Wednesday morning. His headache had become unbearable, and any light or noise made it worse. Ernest drove

St. Joseph Hospital in Memphis. *Courtesy of Memphis Public Library and Information Center.*

him to St. Joseph's Hospital, where doctors determined that Diggs had a concussion caused by his fall two weeks earlier. An X-ray revealed that a steady hemorrhage had caused swelling in his brain.[287]

The orderlies moved Diggs into a room across the hall from his father, where he lingered for a few days, growing weaker until he slipped into a coma. James died the following night without ever regaining consciousness. Still in a coma, Diggs died on Monday morning as doctors prepared for surgery.[288]

Diggs wanted his body donated to the University of Tennessee if he did not make it through surgery. Doctors in the Pathology Department were eager to look for abnormalities in his brain that might explain his criminal tendencies. Diggs had wondered if he had a physical problem that might explain his behavior but shied away from an examination. Ernest, however, could not stand the thought of doctors cutting up his brother. He refused to turn over the body and instead had it interred.[289]

The family gathered with more than one hundred friends at Elmwood Cemetery on Sunday afternoon to say farewell to the picturesque outlaw. Summer was over, and the air had begun to cool. They stood by the side-by-side plots for the father and son as they were laid to rest. Earlier, the

Reverend U.A. Boone had performed services for the two at the McDowell and Monteverde Funeral Home, and he now said some final words. The cemetery provided a final resting place for Memphians from all walks of life. It held mayors and madams, businessmen and laborers, saints and sinners, the remarkable and the ordinary. Diggs Nolen had befriended, annoyed, robbed and helped people from every facet of Memphis society. His family could not have found a more appropriate resting place for him.[290]

Syndicated newspapers from around the country said that Diggs "romped through the world of crime with all the gaiety of a schoolboy on holiday [and] with none of the viciousness of a criminal." Some embellished the details and altered facts to overdramatize his life. Stories began with headlines like "Gang Midas Dies Pauper, Mind Gone," "Man Without a Country Dies After Fall in Memphis" or "How Love Crushed the King of the Memphis Underworld."[291]

The more sensational reporters incorrectly credited Ethel Wikoff, the "queen," with having "toppled the king." In June 1921, Diggs turned down an offer to reconcile when Ethel offered to open a pharmacy with him in El

Scene from Elmwood Cemetery. *Courtesy of Memphis Public Library and Information Center.*

Dorado, Arkansas. Rebuffed, Ethel found a new man to bully and torment. She and Maurice "Morey" Pian married on September 6, 1921, and true to form, she shot and wounded him during an argument in June 1924.[292]

Ethel's dream of leading a gang came true when she married Pian, but her crime spree did not go well. A judge sentenced Ethel to fifteen months in the Rhode Island State Penitentiary after police arrested the couple for narcotics trafficking in March 1922. Pian, whom police called "one of the biggest drug operators in Memphis," was arrested separately on drug charges in July 1923 and again in December 1923.[293]

The couple teamed up with "Boxcar Mike" Beavers to rob a post office in Courtland, Mississippi, on June 19, 1928. Unfortunately for Ethel, things did not go as planned. The robbery went awry and resulted in a shoot-out that left Beavers with a bullet in his leg. Police arrested the three would-be thieves in Memphis.[294]

Local reporters who knew him better described Diggs as unique and colorful. Each recounted his education, pharmacies, exile and prison escapes. Most painted Diggs as mischievous rather than a menace as they speculated on the cause of his downfall.

The grief-stricken Ernest blamed the local businessmen and lawyers who colluded with his brother in the sale of the Liberty bonds stolen by Hart Austin for his downfall. "When he [Diggs] returned to Memphis from prison the last time," said Ernest, "these people frowned on him. They never even sent a wreath to his funeral. These men are now walking the streets free, highly respected people, wealthy, church members." Ernest also claimed that Diggs kept many robbers from operating in Memphis and even thwarted a plan to kill Inspector Will Griffin. Ernest offered no proof, but Mayor Watkins Overton said he would confer with the police and the Shelby County attorney general about the accusations.[295]

Governor Malcolm Patterson, a convert to the cause of Prohibition, believed he knew the reason for Diggs's downfall. According to Patterson,

[Diggs Nolen] *was by no means wholly vicious. He was both generous and kind in his disposition and loyal to those who cared for him. Perhaps he was not always just right mentally, though his mind was bright when not clouded with liquor. The report in this paper that he did not drink was a mistake. Liquor was Nolen's curse. It was the snare that held him fast and ruined what might have been a brilliant and useful life.*[296]

Tom Little of the *Nashville Tennessean* attributed Diggs's downfall his to hero worship of Frank Holloway. He believed Diggs was no different from any other boy in his love of excitement, romance and the lure of heroism. "Fate," Little wrote, "placed an idol in the village to satisfy the boy's thirst for hero worship. Had this idol been a great soldier or statesman or an adventurer of more honorable pursuits than that of highwayman, perhaps the subject for this article might today be sitting in a seat of the high and mighty instead of on a wooden bunk encircled by steel bars."[297]

A year before his death, Diggs blamed politics for his downfall. Little wrote that Diggs, "with all his intelligence, cannot understand that he, with the life he led, was detrimental to politics; that it was the illegal life he led, regardless of whether Madelyn O'Reilly's case against him was authentic, which sent him to the penitentiary." Little noticed that Diggs kept a biography of Robert E. Lee by his bunk in his cell. He suggested that if Diggs turned his hero worship away from Frank Holloway and directed it toward the likes of the Confederate general, he would "march along the straight and narrow."[298]

Diggs Nolen did not live long enough for anyone to see if he would keep his promises about reforming or take responsibility for his actions. One cannot help but wonder if he honestly intended to give up his quixotic quest. The outlaw life had lost its appeal, and his notoriety had become a terrible burden. But was he ready to give it up? Diggs seemed to think so. He told reporters shortly before his death, "I'm through furnishing you stories about me. I've read them all and I know what you write. There have been columns about me and I would sure like to read what kind of stuff you'll put in when I'm gone for good, I mean. It will be the only story about me I that I ever missed."[299]

NOTES

Introduction

1. "Diggs Nolen Isn't Crazy; He Just Wants an Honest Job," *Commercial Appeal* (Memphis, TN), August 28, 1928.
2. "Diggs Nolen Is Dead; Unique Career Ended," *Commercial Appeal* (Memphis, TN), September 3, 1928.
3. Ibid.; Shelby County, death certificate no. 2724 (1928), Henry Diggs Nolen, Shelby County Archives, Shelby County, Tennessee.
4. "Nolen Wanted Body Given to University," *Nashville (TN) Banner*, September 5, 1928.
5. Duncan, "Strange Liking," 3–22.

Chapter 1

6. "Fatal Fire in Memphis," *Camden (TN) Chronicle*, March 31, 1899.
7. "Bryan's Death List Is Four," *Commercial Appeal* (Memphis, TN), March 25, 1899.
8. "Four Suffocated," *Baltimore Sun*, March 25, 1899.
9. "Bryan's Death List."
10. "Fire Takes More Lives," *Rock Island (IA) Argus*, March 25, 1899.

Chapter 2

11. "Below Zero Blast Brings to Chicago Torment for the Poor," *Chicago Tribune*, January 5, 1912; "Slayer Boasts of Crimes," *Evening Times-Republican* (Marshalltown, IO), January 10, 1912.

12. "Confesses to Daring Crimes," *Santa Fe New Mexican*, January 9, 1912; "Man Confesses to Numerous Crimes," *Las Vegas (NV) Optic*, January 10, 1912.

13. "Confesses of Robbing of Banks of $450,000 and Two Murders," *New York Herald*, January 10, 1912.

14. "Slayer Boasts of Crimes," *Evening Times-Republican* (Marshalltown, IO), January 10, 1912.

15. "Former Tulsan Tells of Crimes," *Tulsa (OK) Daily World*, January 10, 1912.

16. Ibid.

17. "Is Here for B.O. Smith," *Pittsburgh Daily Post*, November 18, 1907; "Holloway," *Times-Democrat* (Pawnee, OK), June 18, 1908; "Dead in Tulsa Street Fight," *Cherryvale (OK) Weekly Journal*, June 18, 1908; "Bandits Expected to Free Partner," *Houston (TX) Post*, December 11, 1912.

18. "Shot But Refused to Say Who Did It," *El Paso (TX) Herald*, September 3, 1910; "Bandits Expected."

19. "Confesses to Daring Crimes," *Santa Fe New Mexican*, January 9, 1912; "Pickpocket Kicks In with a Bunch of Thrills," *Albuquerque (NM) Morning Journal*, January 10, 1912.

20. Ibid.

21. "Pickpocket Kicks In"; "Slayer Boasts."

22. "Deadly Desperado Mere Yarn Spinner," *Inter Ocean* (Chicago, IL), January 10, 1912.

23. "Ready to Hang Like a Man," *Carbondale (PA) Daily News*, January 10, 1912.

24. "Confesses Crime for Trip," *Chicago Tribune*, January 10, 1912.

25. "Governor Colquitt Asks for Frank Holloway," *Santa Fe New Mexican*, January 11, 1912; "Texas Bad Man Is Carted Home in Sheriff's Charge," *Inter Ocean* (Chicago, IL), January 18, 1912.

26. "Bank Looter Escapes," *Gazette* (Cedar Rapids, IO), August 5, 1912; "A Notorious Slayer Escapes," *Independence (KS) Daily Reporter*, August 6, 1912; Lucko, "Rusk Penitentiary."

Chapter 3

27. Tom Little, "Did Hero-Worship Make Diggs Nolen a Master of the Underworld?" *Tennessean* (Nashville, TN), August 7, 1927.
28. Biles, *Memphis*, 14; "Police News: The Mayor's Court This Morning Was Full of Scrappers," *Delta-Democrat Times* (Greenville, MS), February 4, 1904; "Nolen Captured in New Orleans," *Chattanooga (TN) Daily Times*, December 11, 1923; "Unique Career Ended."
29. "Diggs Nolen's Downfall Was Caused by Liquor," *Clarion-Ledger* (Jackson, MS), September 21, 1928; Little, "Hero-Worship."
30. "Forger Wanted Here," *Commercial Appeal* (Memphis, TN), November 25, 1912; "Charged with Being a Forger," *Nashville (TN) Banner*, November 25, 1912.
31. "Diggs Nolen in Bad for Texas Forgery," *Omaha (NE) Daily Bee*, December 18, 1912; "Former Tulsa Crook Caught," *Morning Tulsa (OK) Daily World*, December 1, 1912.
32. "Diggs Nolen Makes Plea."
33. "Diggs Is in the Pen," *Topeka (KS) State Journal*, January 22, 1913.
34. "Bold Project of Desperate Men," *Nashville (TN) Banner*, December 11, 1912; Little, "Hero-Worship"; "Former Tulsa Crook Caught."
35. "Ernest Is Held for Trial in Oklahoma," Commercial Appeal (Memphis, TN), February 9, 1913.
36. "Memphis Outs Detective Nolen," *Columbia (TN) Herald*, December 13, 1912.
37. "Bold Project"; "Former Tulsa Crook Caught."
38. Inmate Files of Diggs Nolen, 1913–1917 (24726407) [Electronic Record]; Series: Inmate Case Files, 7/3/1895–11/5/1957, Record Group 129: Records of the Bureau of Prisons, 1870–2009; National Archives at College Park, College Park, MD (retrieved from the Access to Archival Databases at https://catalog.archives.gov/id/24726407, November 27, 2020).
39. Ibid.
40. "Ernest Nolen on Trial," *Nashville (TN) Banner*, February 8, 1913.

Chapter 4

41. Watson, *Walter Malone*, 100–101.
42. "Dead Bandit Was Subject of Poem," *Arkansas Gazette* (Little Rock, AR), December 13, 1912.

43. Bearden, *100 Years*; "Foil a Plan to Rob US Police of a Prisoner," *Leavenworth (KS) Times*, December 11, 1912.

44. "Planned to Free Their Pal," *Nashville Tennessean*, December 11, 1912.

45. "Officers Capture Desperate Gang," *Oxford (MS) Eagle*, December 19, 1912.

46. "Five Bandits Hold Up a Fast Train at Hulburt, Arkansas," *Arkansas Democrat* (Little Rock, AR), February 7, 1912.

47. Ibid.

48. "Foil a Plan."

49. Ibid.

50. Ibid.; "Kinney Bergin Killed," *Baltimore Sun*, December 11, 1912.

51. "Frank Holloway Had Hectic Career Here," *Commercial Appeal* (Memphis, TN), February 9, 1923; "Holloway Shooting Revives Deeds Here," *Commercial Appeal* (Memphis, TN), February 12, 1923.

52. "Ernest L. Nolen Is Dropped from the Force," *Commercial Appeal* (Memphis, TN), December 12, 1912.

53. "Bandits Planned to Kill US Officers and Free Comrade," *Commercial Appeal* (Memphis, TN), December 11, 1912.

54. "Diggs Nolen Starts on His Way to Omaha," *Atlanta (GA) Constitution*, December 2, 1912; "Bold Project."

55. "Outlaws Planned to Liberate Pal," *Hattiesburg (MS) News*, December 11, 1912.

56. "Memphis Outs Detective Nolen," *Columbia (TN) Herald*, December 13, 1912; "Dropped from the Force."

57. "Scandal in the Memphis Police Department," *Chattanooga (TN) Daily Times*, December 12, 1912.

58. "Glycerin Enough to Blow up Block," *Nashville (TN) Banner*, December 11, 1912.

Chapter 5

59. Letter from Ernest L. Nolen to Honorable A.V. Anderson, June 11, 1919, Inmate File of Ernest Nolen, Inmate Case Files, 7/3/1895–11/5/1957, Records of the Bureau of Prisons, 1870–2009, Record Group 129: Records of the Bureau of Prisons, 1870–2009, National Archives Building, Washington, D.C.

60. "Spanish War Vets Are After Land," *Bismarck (ND) Daily Tribune*, October 17, 1909.

61. "Ernest Nolen Given Preliminary Hearing," *Commercial Appeal* (Memphis, TN), February 8, 1913; "Dropped from the Force."

62. "Omaha Court Flushed Gigantic Conspiracy," *Commercial Appeal* (Memphis, TN), February 1, 1913; "Detective Suspended Following Arrests," *Chattanooga (TN) News*, December 10, 1912; "Scandal in the Memphis Police Department," *Chattanooga (TN) Daily Times*, December 12, 1912.

63. "Dropped from the Force."

64. "Omaha Court Flushed"; "Ernest Nolen on Trial," *Nashville (TN) Banner*, February 8, 1913.

65. "Ernest Nolen Given Preliminary Hearing," *Commercial Appeal* (Memphis, TN), February 8, 1913; "Nolen's Brother in Toils," *Omaha (NE) Daily Bee*, February 2, 1913.

66. "Diggs Nolen Makes Plea of Not Guilty in Munger's Court," *Omaha (NE) Daily Bee*, December 21, 1912; "Jail Escape Is Frustrated," *Omaha (NE) Daily Bee*, January 8, 1913.

67. "Charged with Conspiracy," *Times-Democrat* (New Orleans, LA), February 1, 1913; "John Jones Goes Back upon Nolen on Stand," *Omaha (NE) Daily Bee*, February 9, 1913.

68. "Cellmate of Diggs Nolen Held to the Federal Jury," *Omaha (NE) Daily Bee*, January 23, 1913; "Jail Escape Is Frustrated," *Omaha (NE) Daily Bee*, January 8, 1913.

69. "Diggs Is in Pen," *Topeka (KS) State Journal*, January 22, 1913; "Diggs Nolen Guilty," *Commercial Appeal* (Memphis, TN), January 12, 1913.

70. "Nolen and Jones Arrested in Memphis," *Omaha (NE) Daily Bee*, February 1, 1913; "Nolen's Brother in Toils"; "Ernest Nolen Given Preliminary Hearing," *Commercial Appeal* (Memphis, TN), February 8, 1913; "Ernest Nolen on Trial," *Nashville (TN) Banner*, February 8, 1913.

71. "Prisoner Heavily Guarded," *Bedford (IN) Daily Mail*, February 22, 1913; "Ernest Is Held for Trial in Oklahoma," Commercial Appeal (Memphis, TN), February 9, 1913.

72. "Ernest Nolen Off to Pen," *McNairy County Independent.* (Selmer, TN), April 18, 1913; "Ernest Nolen Pardoned," *Commercial Appeal* (Memphis, TN), October 9, 1913.

73. "Mrs. Diggs Nolen Wanted," *Commercial Appeal* (Memphis, TN), April 1, 1913; "Federal Authorities May Bring Ethel Nolen Back," *Omaha (NE) Daily Bee*, April 3, 1913; "Mrs. Nolen Arrested," *Commercial Appeal* (Memphis, TN), April 2, 1913; "Ethel Nolen Brought Back to Omaha for Trial," *Omaha (NE) Daily Bee*, April 4, 1913.

Chapter 6

74. "Morgan Declines to Be Prison Warden," *Lansing (KS) News*, January 3, 1913; "Thomas W. Morgan Warden at Leavenworth," *Chattanooga (TN) Daily Times*, June 4, 1913; Connelley, *Standard History*; "Biography of Thomas W. Morgan," AccessGenealogy, https://accessgenealogy.com/kansas/biography-of-thomas-w-morgan.htm

75. "Tom Morgan at Atlanta," *Leavenworth (KS) Weekly Times*, June 12, 1913; "Morgan May Go to Washington to See M'Reynolds," *Leavenworth (KS) Times*, January 29, 1914.

76. "Government Will Give Free Legal Aid to Convicts," *Leavenworth (KS) Weekly Times*, February 12, 1914.

77. "Saw Bars and Escape from Federal Prison," *Ottawa (KS) Daily Republic*, June 30, 1913.

78. "Former Editor Is Proving an Able Prison Keeper," *Leavenworth (KS) Times*, July 15, 1914.

79. U.S. Penitentiary Record of Diggs Nolen, Inmate File of Diggs Nolen, Inmate Case Files, 7/3/1895–11/5/1957, Hospital Records of Diggs Nolen, January 12, 1913, August 18, 1917, and Physical Examination of Prisoner, January 12, 1913, U.S. Penitentiary Record of Diggs Nolen, Inmate File of Diggs Nolen, Inmate Case Files, 7/3/1895–11/5/1957, Records of the Bureau of Prisons, 1870–2009, Record Group 129: Records of the Bureau of Prisons, 1870–2009, National Archives Building, Washington, D.C.

80. Record of Diggs Nolen, 1913–1916, Inmate File of Diggs Nolen, National Archives.

81. Letter from CPJ Mooney to Thomas Morgan, February 17, 1914, Letter from W.L. Kearney to Thomas Morgan, December 3, 1913, Inmate File of Diggs Nolen, National Archives.

82. Letter from Thomas Morgan to Luke Lea, May 8, 1914, Letter from Diggs Nolen to John Sharp Williams, July 22, 1914, Inmate File of Diggs Nolen, National Archives.

83. "Ernest Nolen Off to Pen," *McNairy County Independent* (Selmer, TN), April 18, 1913; Letter from Thomas Morgan to Ella Nolen, August 11, 1913, Inmate File of Diggs Nolen, National Archives.

84. Letter from F.S. Howell to R.W. McClaughry, April 14, 1913, Inmate File of Diggs Nolen, National Archives.

85. Speaker, "Revealing Data."

86. Letter from Ella Nolen to Diggs Nolen, July 24, 1914, Inmate File of Diggs Nolen, National Archives.
87. Letter from Diggs Nolen to Luke Lea, July 3, 1914, and letter from Diggs Nolen to John Sharp Williams, July 22, 1914, Inmate File of Diggs Nolen, National Archives.

Chapter 7

88. "Nolen Escapes Prison," *Omaha (NE) Evening Bee*, July 23, 1914.
89. Letter from Ernest Nolen to Thomas Morgan, November 24, 1914, Inmate File of Diggs Nolen, National Archives; "Captive Identified as Floyd Nolen," *Daily Arkansas Gazette* (Little Rock, AR), January 30, 1915.
90. Telegram from Thomas Morgan to William McElveen, January 18, 1915, Inmate File of Diggs Nolen, National Archives.
91. Letter from Thomas Morgan to US Attorney General, July 23, 1914, Inmate File of Diggs Nolen, National Archives.
92. Letter from J.A. Connelly to Thomas Morgan, February 26, 1915, Inmate File of Diggs Nolen, National Archives.
93. "Houston Daylight Bank Robbery," *Bryan (TX) Daily Eagle and Pilot*, January 27, 1915; "Trail of Coin Thru Street Causes Arrest," *Daily Ardmoreite* (Ardmore, OK), January 27, 1915; "Bank Robbers Identified," *Daily Ardmoreite* (Ardmore, OK), January 28, 1915; Letter from Horace Dale to Thomas Morgan, March 6, 1915, Inmate File of Diggs Nolen, National Archives.
94. "Bank Robber Identified," *Batesville (AR) Guard*, February 19, 1915.
95. Telegram from Thomas Morgan to New Orleans Chief of Police, July 24, 1914, Inmate File of Diggs Nolen, National Archives.
96. Letter from Ella Nolen to Thomas Morgan, February 19, 1915, letter from Thomas Morgan to Ella Nolen, February 25, 1915, correspondence, February 1915, letter from Ella Nolen to Thomas Morgan, November 8, 1915, Inmate File of Diggs Nolen, National Archives.
97. Letter from Helen Rosser to Thomas Morgan, May 17, 1915, letter from Thomas Morgan to Helen Rosser, June 3, 1915, Inmate File of Diggs Nolen, National Archives.
98. Telegram from Helen Rosser to Diggs Nolen, March 31, 1917, Inmate File of Diggs Nolen, National Archives.

99. Telegram from Diggs Nolen to Helen Rosser, May 16, 1917, telegram from Helen Rosser to Diggs Nolen, May 17, 1917, Inmate File of Diggs Nolen, National Archives.

100. Letter from Luke Lea to Thomas Morgan, January 26, 1916, telegram from Diggs Nolen to Luke Lea, September 1, 1916, U.S. Penitentiary Record of Diggs Nolen, Inmate File of Diggs Nolen, National Archives.

101. Telegram from Diggs Nolen to Bob O'Rourke, December 7, 1917, letter from Diggs Nolen to Thomas Morgan, January 15, 1918, U.S. Penitentiary Record of Diggs Nolen, Inmate File of Diggs Nolen, National Archives.

Chapter 8

102. Marion and Oliver, "Harrison Narcotics Act (1914)," in *Drugs in American Society*, 470–73; "An End to Dope Trade," *Chattanooga (TN) Daily Times*, February 10, 1915.

103. Marion and Oliver; "Memphis Hospital for Drug Victims," *Nashville (TN) Banner*, March 9, 1914.

104. "Crusade Is Begun on Indiscriminant [*sic*] Dope Prescription," *Yazoo (MS) Herald*, May 28, 1915; "Three Thousand Stamps Issued," *Nashville (TN) Banner*, March 6, 1914.

105. Courtwright, Joseph and Des Jarlais, *Addicts Who Survived*, 6–10; "Cinema of Crime Reflected on Police Blotter," *News Scimitar* (Memphis, TN), December 19, 1919.

106. Biles, *Memphis*, 16; Miller, *Memphis*, 91; Lauterbach, *Beale Street Dynasty*, 126–27; "Dope Meet Today," *Commercial Appeal* (Memphis, TN), August 31, 1922; "Drug Problem Up to Mayor Paine Today," *Commercial Appeal* (Memphis, TN), September 9, 1922; "County Favors Plan to Aid Drug Addicts," *Commercial Appeal* (Memphis, TN), September 13, 1922; "Propose Drug Addict Home," *Commercial Appeal* (Memphis, TN), October 28, 1922.

107. "2443 Known Drug Users," *Chattanooga (TN) Daily Times*, January 8, 1915.

108. "Memphis Hospital for Drug Victims"; "Dr. Brown on Drug Situation," *Nashville (TN) Banner*, March 6, 1914.

109. "Question Must Be Decided: Can You Get Drunk on 2.75?" *New York Tribune*, June 15, 1919.

110. "Calls Memphis Narcotic Center of United States," *Tulsa (OK) Daily World*, August 11, 1918; "Designates Memphis as Center of Dope Traffic," *Chattanooga (TN) News*, August 10, 1918; "Two Women Have $12,000 in Drugs," *Daily Arkansas Gazette* (Little Rock, AR), November 30, 1918.
111. "City Takes Pity on Drug Addicts," *News Scimitar* (Memphis, TN), October 24, 1919.
112. "Lt. Corey Better, Pians Held by Poole," *Commercial Appeal* (Memphis, TN), November 1, 1921.
113. "Young Girl Found with Two Brothers," *Kingfisher (OK) Daily Free Press*, March 6, 1915; "Women Released," *Daily Arkansas Gazette* (Little Rock, AR), March 8, 1919.
114. "$12,000 in Drugs"; "Floyd Nolen in the Toils Again," *Daily Arkansas Gazette* (Little Rock, AR), April 14, 1920; "Two Years in the Pen for Floyd Nolen," *Daily Arkansas Gazette* (Little Rock, AR), June 16 ,1920.
115. "New Time Card Issued", *Commercial Appeal* (Memphis, TN), November 16, 1918.
116. "Wholesale Drugs Not Restricted," *Daily Arkansas Gazette* (Little Rock, AR), December 1, 1918.
117. "Two Years in the Pen."
118. "$12,000 in Drugs."
119. "Wholesale Drugs Not Restricted."
120. Ibid.
121. Ibid.; "Two Years in the Pen."
122. "Young Women Say They Are Lucky to Be in Jail," *Daily Arkansas Gazette* (Little Rock, AR), January 4, 1919.
123. "Women Released"; "Nolen Brothers Facing Serious Arkansas Charges," *News Scimitar* (Memphis, TN), May 2, 1919.

Chapter 9

124. "Police Take Four Suspects in Raid," *Commercial Appeal* (Memphis, TN), July 2, 1919.
125. "Say Woman Had Liquor," *Commercial Appeal* (Memphis, TN), July 3, 1919; "Four Suspects Are Arrested in Raid by Police," *News Scimitar* (Memphis, TN), July 1, 1919.
126. "Three Men Held on Charge of Robbing Humboldt Post Office," *News Scimitar* (Memphis, TN), July 2, 1919.

127. "Ethel Wyckoff Held on Liquor Charge," *News Scimitar* (Memphis, TN), July 3, 1919; "Briggs, Infamous, Reinstated, Booze Seller Set Free," *News Scimitar* (Memphis, TN), July 11, 1919; "Another Case Lost by Quinn Appointee," *News Scimitar* (Memphis, TN), July 26, 1919.
128. Little, "Hero-Worship"; "How Love Crushed the King of the Memphis Underworld," *Pittsburgh (PA) Sun-Telegraph*, September 23, 1928.
129. "Gang Midas Dies Pauper, Mind Gone," *Daily News* (New York, NY), September 4, 1928; "Catches Accused as Bank Bandit," *News Scimitar* (Memphis, TN), October 1, 1919; "Suspected Robbing Bank at Collierville," *Commercial Appeal* (Memphis, TN), July 22, 1920; "W.J. O'Neal Held," *Commercial Appeal* (Memphis, TN), July 22, 1920.
130. "Continue Austin Case," *Commercial Appeal* (Memphis, TN), August 28, 1920; "Austin, Held in NC, Called Real Bad Man," *Commercial Appeal* (Memphis, TN), October 1, 1933; "Collierville Bank Robbed of $75,000," *Commercial Appeal* (Memphis, TN), February 27, 1920; "Bank Offers Two Thousand Dollar Reward for Bandits," *Commercial Appeal* (Memphis, TN), February 28, 1920.
131. "Bank Offers Two Thousand Dollar Reward for Bandits," *Commercial Appeal* (Memphis, TN), February 28, 1920.
132. "Diggs Nolen Is Dead," *Evening World-Herald* (Omaha, NE), September 8, 1928.

Chapter 10

133. "Diggs Nolen Has Bunch of Voters for Mr. Williams," *News Scimitar* (Memphis), October 17, 1919.
134. Phillips, "Rowlett Paine," 95–99; Sigafoos, *Cotton Row*, 122–23.
135. Biles, *Memphis*, 19.
136. "Diggs Nolen Indicted," *Commercial Appeal* (Memphis, TN), October 29, 1919; "Bates Must Decide What to Do with Nolen Evidence," *News Scimitar* (Memphis), October 27, 1919.
137. "Diggs Nolen Has Bunch"; "Election Crookedness," *News Scimitar* (Memphis), October 28, 1919; "Paine and Progress or Williams and Reaction?" *Commercial Appeal* (Memphis, TN), November 2, 1919; Rowlett Paine Collection, Citizens' League of Memphis Platform, 1919, Misc. Documents, Box 33/39.
138. "New Methods or Old Only Issue Before Voters," *News Scimitar* (Memphis), November 6, 1919.

139. "Nolen Is Arrested Again," *News Scimitar* (Memphis), November 6, 1919.

140. "New Methods."

141. Dowdy, *Mayor Crump*, 30–31; "Victory for Righteousness Won Mainly by the Women," *News Scimitar* (Memphis, TN), November 7, 1919.

142. "Diggs Nolen Arrested," *Commercial Appeal* (Memphis, TN), January 17, 1920; "Diggs Nolen Landed on Same Old Charge," *News Scimitar* (Memphis), January 20, 1920; "Begin Trial of Diggs Nolen Suit," *News Scimitar* (Memphis), June 1, 1920.

143. "Diggs Nolen Shot; Mrs. Nolen Arrested," *Commercial Appeal* (Memphis, TN) March 15, 1920; "Mrs. Nolen Files Suit," *Commercial Appeal* (Memphis, TN), June 26, 1920.

144. "Mrs. Nolen Files Suit."

145. "Nolen Case Jury Failure Angers Justice McCall," *News Scimitar* (Memphis, TN), June 2, 1920.

146. "Hung Jury in Nolen Trial in US Court," *Little Rock Daily News* (Little Rock, AR), June 16, 1920; "Jury Disagrees in Diggs Nolen Case," *Daily Arkansas Gazette* (Little Rock, AR), June 17, 1920.

147. "Federal Jury Fails to Convict Druggist," *Commercial Appeal* (Memphis, TN), February 3, 1921.

148. "Nolen Must Pay Big Sum for Tax Evasion," *News Scimitar* (Memphis, TN), June 19, 1920; "Claim Diggs Nolen Dodged Income Tax," *Commercial Appeal* (Memphis, TN), June 19, 1920.

149. "Four Now in Custody in Liberty Bonds Case," *Commercial Appeal* (Memphis, TN), February 5, 1921.

150. "Drug Store Seized," *Commercial Appeal* (Memphis, TN), February 22, 1922; "Druggist Accused of Juggling Income Tax," *New York Tribune*, February 8, 1921.

Chapter 11

151. Sutch, "Liberty Bonds."

152. "Hold Up Two Bond Runners, Escape in Car with $466,000," *New York Herald*, December 1, 1920.

153. "Sought as Bond Hold-Up Chief, He Surrenders," *New York Tribune*, February 11, 1921; "Vanelli Held in $50,000 Bail in Big Bond Theft," *New York Tribune*, February 12, 1921.

154. "Two Bond Runners."

155. "Youth Confesses Part in $466,000 Bond Theft Plot," *Daily News* (New York, NY), December 2, 1920; "Daring Bandits Get $466,000 Loot," *Daily News* (New York, NY), December 1, 1920.

156. "466,000 Bond Theft Cleared, Police Assert," *New York Tribune*, December 2, 1920.

157. "Two Bond Runners"; "Daring Bandits."

158. "2 Confess Part in $466,000 Bond Robbery," *New York Tribune*, April 2, 1921; "Diggs Nolen Is Dead," *Evening World-Herald* (Omaha, NE), September 28, 1928.

159. "Sold Bonds from $466,000 Holdup," *New York Herald*, April 2, 1921; "Confession Alleged in Stolen Bonds Case," *Commercial Appeal* (Memphis, TN), April 2, 1921; "Mastermind in Theft of Bonds Is Still Sought," *Vicksburg (MS) Evening Post*, February 5, 1921; "Bond Theft Case Narrowing Down," *Pensacola (FL) Journal*, February 7, 1921; "Stolen Liberty Bonds Located in Memphis," *Lexington (TN) Progress*, February 11, 1921.

160. "Duffy Is Back," *Commercial Appeal* (Memphis, TN), April 26, 1921.

161. "Four Now in Custody in Liberty Bonds Case," *Commercial Appeal* (Memphis, TN), February 5, 1921; "Druggist Accused of Juggling Income Tax," *New York Tribune*, February 8, 1921.

162. "Six Are Indicted in Stolen Bond Case," *North Mississippi Herald* (Water Valley, MS), February 25, 1921; "El Dorado Deputies Take Man with Gem," *Commercial Appeal* (Memphis, TN), July 30, 1923; "Stolen Liberty Bonds Located in Memphis," *Lexington (TN) Progress*, February 11, 1921; "Mastermind in Theft."

163. "Four Arrested in $400,000 Robbery," *New York Herald*, February 5, 1921.

164. "$255,000 Bond Theft Traced; Four Arrested," *New York Tribune*, February 5, 1921; "Six Are Indicted"; "Four Arrested."

165. "Memphis Banker Will Face Court," *Atlanta (GA) Constitution*, February 9, 1921; "Stolen Liberty Bonds Located."

166. "Banker Is Held in Bond Stealing," *Pensacola (FL) Journal*, February 5, 1921; "Sues Judge's Son Over Sale of Stolen Bonds," *Brooklyn Daily Eagle* (New York, NY), June 3, 1922; "Identify Anderson in Liberty Bond Case," *Commercial Appeal* (Memphis, TN), November 19, 1925.

167. "Shelby Grand Jury Acts in Bond Deal," *Covington (TN) Leader*, March 3, 1921; "Sensations Promised in Liberty Bond Deal," *Commercial Appeal* (Memphis, TN), February 6, 1921; "Objects to Trial with Diggs Nolen," *Covington (TN) Leader*, April 14, 1921; "Cases Will Be Split," *Commercial Appeal* (Memphis, TN), April 10, 1921.

168. "Important Arrest in Bond Case Is Made," *Commercial Appeal* (Memphis, TN), March 3, 1921; "Confession Alleged in Stolen Bonds Case," *Commercial Appeal* (Memphis, TN), April 2, 1921; "Duffy Is Back."

Chapter 12

169. "H. Diggs Nolen Shot in Brawl with Wife," *Commercial Appeal* (Memphis, TN), February 21, 1921; "Drugstore Owner Shot by His Wife," *Bridgeport (CT) Times and Evening Farmer*, February 21, 1921; "Love Crushed the King."

170. "Shot in Brawl."

171. "Nolen Arrested Again," *Commercial Appeal* (Memphis, TN), February 17, 1921; "Nolen Scores Once," *Commercial Appeal* (Memphis, TN), February 15, 1921; "Four Now in Custody in Liberty Bonds Case," *Commercial Appeal* (Memphis, TN), February 5, 1921; "H. Diggs Nolen Shot."

172. "Four Now in Custody"; "Druggist Shot by His Wife," *Pensacola (FL) Journal*, February 22, 1921; "Indicted Druggist Shot," *Topeka (KS) State Journal*, February 21, 1921.

173. "Drug Store Seized," *Commercial Appeal* (Memphis, TN), February 22, 1922.

174. Ibid.

175. "Diggs Nolen Better," *Commercial Appeal* (Memphis, TN), February 23, 1921.

176. "First Stolen Bond Cases Go to Trial," *Commercial Appeal* (Memphis, TN), April 26, 1921; "Technicality May Stop Bond Cases," *North Mississippi Herald* (Water Valley, MS), April 29, 1921.

177. "Nolen and Huntley Easily Acquitted," *North Mississippi Herald* (Water Valley, MS), May 6, 1921.

178. Ibid.

179. "Omaha Man Is Freed in Bond Case," *Omaha (NE) Daily Bee*, May 4, 1921; "Shelby Grand Jury Acts in Bond Deal," *Covington (TN) Leader*, March 3, 1921.

180. "Diggs Nolen Sues Wife for Divorce," *Winona (MS) Times*, April 22, 1921.

181. "Ethel Has Respite," *Commercial Appeal* (Memphis, TN), May 25, 1921.

182. "H. Diggs Nolen Gets Divorce from Ethel," *North Mississippi Herald* (Water Valley, MS), May 27, 1921.

Chapter 13

183. "May Not Push Claim," *Commercial Appeal* (Memphis, TN), March 2, 1921; "Nolen's Income Tax Dispute Is Settled," *Commercial Appeal* (Memphis, TN), April 5, 1921.

184. "Two Officers Shot to Death by Hold Up Men," *Chattanooga (TN) Daily Times*, August 11, 1921.

185. Ibid.

186. "Memphis Cleanup Planned After Three Slain in Holdup," *St. Louis (MO) Globe-Democrat*, August 11, 1921; "Diggs Nolen Will Try Life on Farm," *Nashville (TN) Banner*, August 17, 1921; "Diggs Nolen Bids Memphis Farewell," *Omaha (NE) Daily Bee*, August 18, 1921.

187. "Wanted Partner with $5000 Cash for Drugstore," *Commercial Appeal* (Memphis, TN), June 2, 1921; "Diggs Nolen and Former Wife to Forget Stormy Past, It Is Said," *Arkansas Democrat* (Little Rock, AR), June 3, 1921.

188. "Chemical Company's License Forfeited," *Tennessean* (Nashville, TN), July 7, 1921; "Law Destroys Illicit Liquor," *Arkansas Democrat* (Little Rock, AR), August 31, 1921; "Rum Runners Fined and Turned Loose," *Arkansas Democrat* (Little Rock, AR), August 31, 1921.

189. "Police Raid Diggs Nolen's Drugstore," *Commercial Appeal* (Memphis, TN), July 27, 1921; "Nolen Walks Out of Court Free," *Commercial Appeal* (Memphis, TN), March 3, 1922.

190. "To My Creditors," *Commercial Appeal* (Memphis, TN), September 10, 1921.

191. "Nolens to Remain," *Commercial Appeal* (Memphis, TN), September 17, 1921.

192. "Diggs Pleads Guilty," *Commercial Appeal* (Memphis, TN), September 12, 1921; "In Bankruptcy, Diggs Takes a Trip North," *Commercial Appeal* (Memphis, TN), September 10, 1921.

Chapter 14

193. "A Letter to the Public from H. Diggs Nolen," *Commercial Appeal* (Memphis, TN), May 20, 1922.

194. "Diggs's Cut-Rate Drugstore, by Diggs Nolen," *Commercial Appeal* (Memphis, TN), May 26, 1922.

195. Ibid; "Diggs Nolen Is Dead," *Evening World-Herald*.

196. "Third Letter Advertisement, by Diggs Nolen," *Commercial Appeal* (Memphis, TN), June 6, 1922.

197. "Diggs Nolen Is Arrested on Narcotic Charge," *Commercial Appeal* (Memphis, TN), June 17, 1922; "Arrest Diggs' Father on Narcotic Charge," *Commercial Appeal* (Memphis, TN), July 24, 1922.

198. "Fourth Letter—Advertisement, Digg Nolen's Cut Rate Drug Store, by Diggs," *Commercial Appeal* (Memphis, TN), June 17, 1922; "Diggs Nolen Held," *Commercial Appeal* (Memphis, TN), June 18, 1922.

199. "Finds Diggs Nolen Guilty of Forgery," *Nashville (TN) Banner*, December 9, 1922.

200. "H. Diggs Nolen Found Guilty of Forgery Charge," *Tennessean* (Nashville, TN), December 9, 1922; "In Bankruptcy, Diggs Nolen Takes a Trip North," *Commercial Appeal* (Memphis, TN), September 10, 1921; "Diggs Again," *Commercial Appeal* (Memphis, TN), August 5, 1922.

201. "Ohio Marriages, 1800–1958," FamilySearch database, accessed December 8, 2014, Henry D. Nolen and Margaret May Haring, 04 Sep 1922; citing, Butler, Ohio, reference 2:3JLJR7N; FHL microfilm 355, 794; "Twice in One Day for Diggs," *Commercial Appeal* (Memphis, TN), September 13, 1922; "Pugilist Is Wounded in Shooting Affray," *Commercial Appeal* (Memphis, TN), September 30, 1922.

202. "Hart Austin Again Nabbed by Police," *Commercial Appeal* (Memphis, TN), August 28, 1921; "Diggs Nolen Faces Charge of Forgery," *Commercial Appeal* (Memphis, TN), December 8, 1922.

203. "Diggs Nolen, Educated Convict Says Law Is Hard to Beat," *Tennessean* (Nashville, TN), July 9, 1927; Little, "Hero-Worship."

204. "Twice in One Day."

Chapter 15

205. "Whisky and Plumage Cause Greek's Arrest," *Commercial Appeal* (Memphis, TN), August 9, 1922.

206. Ibid.

207. "Pugilist Shot in Restaurant Brawl," *Knoxville (TN) News Sentinel*, September 30, 1922; Little, "Hero-Worship."

208. Ibid.

209. "Pugilist Is Wounded in Shooting Affray," *Commercial Appeal* (Memphis, TN), September 30, 1922.

210. "Forfeit Nolen Bonds," *Commercial Appeal* (Memphis, TN), November 16, 1922; "Diggs Nolen Ill," *Commercial Appeal* (Memphis, TN), February 21, 1923; "Andrews Meets Coleman at SAC Monday Night," *Commercial Appeal* (Memphis, TN), September 27, 1925.

211. "They Don't Want Diggs," *Winona (MS) Times*, November 24, 1922; "Don't Want Diggs," *Commercial Appeal* (Memphis, TN), November 18, 1922.

212. "Nolen Still in Jail," *Commercial Appeal* (Memphis, TN), November 23, 1922; "Jury Says H.D. Nolen Raised Wife's Check," *Commercial Appeal* (Memphis, TN) December 9, 1922; "H. Diggs Nolen Found Guilty of Forgery Charge," *Tennessean* (Nashville, TN), December 9, 1922.

213. "Nolen Eludes Capture by Officers," *Commercial Appeal* (Memphis, TN), December 8, 1923.

214. "Diggs Is Ill; Fighting Drug Habit," *Commercial Appeal* (Memphis, TN), January 30, 1923.

215. Ibid.

216. "Frank Holloway Had Hectic Career Here," *Commercial Appeal* (Memphis, TN), February 9, 1923.

217. "Diggs Nolen Says He Knows Who Killed Noted Bandit," *Arkansas Democrat* (Little Rock, AR), February 9, 1923.

218. "Diggs Nolen Arrested," *Commercial Appeal* (Memphis, TN), March 30, 1923; Ella Brantley Nolan, State of Tennessee, State Board of Health, Bureau of Vital Statistics, Certificate of Death, file 1675, May 31, 1923.

219. "Ernest—Diggs at Outs," *Commercial Appeal* (Memphis, TN), June 23, 1923.

220. "Druggist Held After Attempt to Pass Check," *Winona (MS) Times*, June 15, 1923; "Draft Turned Down; Mississippian Held," *Commercial Appeal* (Memphis, TN), June 9, 1923.

221. "Druggist Held After Attempt."

222. "Ernest Bell Scored by Judge Fitzhugh," *Commercial Appeal* (Memphis, TN), June 10, 1923; "Says Mr. Bell, 'Did You Lecture Me?' Says Mr. Fitzhugh. 'Positively Not!'" *Commercial Appeal* (Memphis, TN), June 13, 1923.

223. "Diggs Nolen Convicted," *Commercial Appeal* (Memphis, TN), June 15, 1923; "Diggs Nolen to Serve Five Years," *Winona (MS) Times*, June 22, 1923.

224. "Diggs to Serve 5 Years in US Prison," *Commercial Appeal* (Memphis, TN), June 19, 1923.

225. "Fitzhugh Enthusiastic," *Commercial Appeal* (Memphis, TN), October 30, 1923.

226. "Election Struggle Enters Last Phases," *Commercial Appeal* (Memphis, TN), October 30, 1923.

227. Little, "Hero-Worship."

Chapter 16

228. "Day by Day with Gov. Patterson," *Commercial Appeal* (Memphis, TN), December 11, 1923.

229. "Noted Prisoner Makes Getaway," *Chattanooga (TN) Daily Times*, December 7, 1923; "Nolen Seeks Release from Pen," *Commercial Appeal* (Memphis, TN), October 16, 1927.

230. "Diggs Nolen Escapes Clutch of Uncle Sam," *Commercial Appeal* (Memphis, TN), December 7, 1923; "Diggs Nolen, Ex-Omahan, Is Again Missing," *Omaha (NE) Daily Bee*, December 15, 1923.

231. "Nolen Here to Tell Grand Jury of Dope," *Commercial Appeal* (Memphis, TN), December 6, 1923; "Noted Prisoner Makes Getaway," *Chattanooga (TN) Daily Times*, December 7, 1923.

232. "Diggs Nolen Eludes Capture by Officers," *Commercial Appeal* (Memphis, TN), December 8, 1923.

233. "Stage Raid on Mulcahy," *Commercial Appeal* (Memphis, TN), December 8, 1923; "Diggs Nolen Sighted but Makes Getaway," *Chattanooga (TN) Daily Times*, December 8, 1923; "Nolen Still Refuses to Give Himself Up," *Commercial Appeal* (Memphis, TN), December 9, 1923.

234. "Nolen Is Caught by New Orleans Police," *Commercial Appeal* (Memphis, TN), December 11, 1923.

235. "Diggs Nolen Held at New Orleans," *Nashville (TN) Banner*, December 11, 1923.

236. "Nolen Captured in New Orleans," *Chattanooga (TN) Daily Times*, December 11, 1923.

237. "Prepare to Return Prisoner to Memphis," *Chattanooga (TN) Daily Times*, December 14, 1923; "Diggs Is Coming Back," *Commercial Appeal* (Memphis, TN), December 12, 1923; "Nolen, Educated Convict."

238. "Narcotic Agent to Be Stationed Here," *Commercial Appeal* (Memphis, TN), August 31, 1922; *Commercial Appeal* (Memphis, TN), September 1, 1922; "Frazier Gives Bond, Leaves for El Paso," *Commercial Appeal* (Memphis, TN), September 24, 1922; "Frazier Is Acquitted of Van Spring Murder," *Commercial Appeal* (Memphis, TN), January 13, 1923.

239. "Diggs Nolen in Back as Federal Witness," *Commercial Appeal* (Memphis, TN), May 28, 1924.
240. "Diggs Nolen Again in Custody of Sheriff; 10 of 41 Back in Jail," *Commercial Appeal* (Memphis, TN), June 24, 1924; "Jailer Says Diggs Is but a Troublemaker," *Commercial Appeal* (Memphis, TN), June 25, 1924.
241. "41 Prisoners Dig Way to Freedom in Record County Jail Delivery," *Commercial Appeal* (Memphis, TN), June 24, 1924.
242. "Diggs Nolen Again."
243. "Jailer Says Diggs."
244. "Diggs Nolen Again."
245. "It Flattened Out," *Commercial Appeal* (Memphis, TN), June 28, 1924.
246. "Diggs Nolen Again"; "Jailer Says Diggs."
247. "Diggs Nolen Again."
248. Ibid.
249. "Nolo Contendre Plea Made by Wilkersons," *Commercial Appeal* (Memphis, TN), July 1, 1924.
250. "Jailer Says."
251. "Nolo Contendre Plea."
252. Ibid.
253. Ibid.
254. "Discharge Guard Who Let Diggs Escape," *Commercial Appeal* (Memphis, TN), March 16, 1925; "Diggs Steps Down," *Commercial Appeal* (Memphis, TN), March 17, 1925.

Chapter 17

255. Little, "Hero-Worship."
256. "Plan Fight to Keep Diggs from Prison," *Commercial Appeal* (Memphis, TN), June 18, 1926.
257. "Nolen, Educated Convict."
258. Ibid.
259. "State Is Combing for Fleeing Convict Gang," *Commercial Appeal* (Memphis, TN), April 11, 1926; "Nolen Parole Story Draws Ire of Paine," *Commercial Appeal* (Memphis, TN), June 22, 1926.
260. "Paine Protest Balks Diggs Nolen Parole," *Commercial Appeal* (Memphis, TN), June 24, 1926.
261. "Lions' Club Indorses Fight Against Nolen," *Commercial Appeal* (Memphis, TN), June 23, 1926.

262. "State Will Lose Its Hold on Nolen Today, *Commercial Appeal* (Memphis, TN), July 8, 1927; "Diggs Nolen Parole Hits Temporary Snag," *Commercial Appeal* (Memphis, TN), July 7, 1927; "Diggs Nolen Located Here and Is Arrested," *Commercial Appeal* (Memphis, TN), November 17, 1927; "Nolen's Exile Contest Is Continued," *Commercial Appeal* (Memphis, TN), November 22, 1927; "Diggs Nolen Gets Parole," *Nashville Tennessean*, July 8, 1927.

263. "Diggs Nolen Gets Parole," *Nashville Tennessean*, July 8, 1927; Little, "Hero-Worship"; "US Gets Diggs Nolen," *Commercial Appeal* (Memphis, TN), July 29, 1927.

264. Telegram from Charles M. Bryan to Diggs Nolen, Inmate file of H. Diggs Nolen, Inmate Case files 7/3/1895–11/5/1957, Records of the Bureau of Prisons, 1870–2007, National Archives at Kansas City, MO; "Nolen Seeks Release."

265. "Diggs Nolen Is Again on Outside of Prison," *Commercial Appeal* (Memphis, TN), November 1, 1927.

266. "Bossism to Remain Issue, Says Mayor," *Commercial Appeal* (Memphis, TN), November 1, 1927.

267. "Diggs Nolen Located Here and Arrested," *Commercial Appeal* (Memphis, TN), November 17, 1927.

268. "Nolen's Exile Contest Is Continued," *Commercial Appeal* (Memphis, TN), November 22, 1927.

269. "Diggs Nolen's Fate to Be Decided Today," *Commercial Appeal* (Memphis, TN), November 29, 1927.

270. "Diggs Nolen Returns After His Day's Exile," *Commercial Appeal* (Memphis, TN), November 30, 1927.

271. "Diggs Nolen Has One More Week to Credit," *News Scimitar* (Memphis, TN), December 4, 1927; "Nolen to Ask Horton If He Is Exile or Not," *Commercial Appeal* (Memphis, TN), December 6, 1927.

272. "Nolen Loses First Freedom Fight Step," *Commercial Appeal* (Memphis, TN), December 1, 1927; "Nolen to Ask Horton," *Commercial Appeal* (Memphis, TN), December 6, 1927; "Delay Decision Again in H. Diggs Nolen Case," *Commercial Appeal* (Memphis, TN), December 15, 1927.

Chapter 18

273. "Nolen Is in Again," *Commercial Appeal* (Memphis, TN), January 1, 1928.

274. "Diggs Nolen in Again," *Commercial Appeal* (Memphis, TN), January 11, 1928.

275. "How Mrs. Buchan Trapped the Hiding Desperado," *San Francisco Examiner*, January 11, 1925.

276. "Bank Yegg Freed by Court in SL Again in Trouble," *Deseret News* (Salt Lake City, UT), March 7, 1928.

277. "Austin, Held in NC."

278. "Diggs Nolen Picked Up by Police Again," *Commercial Appeal* (Memphis, TN), March 9, 1928.

279. "Diggs Nolen Is in Again; Is Accused by Landlady," *Commercial Appeal* (Memphis, TN), June 3, 1928; "Diggs Nolen Is Indicted," *Commercial Appeal* (Memphis, TN), June 16, 1928.

280. "Diggs Nolen Isn't Crazy."

281. "Nolen Visits Friends," *News Scimitar* (Memphis, TN), July 24, 1919; Letter from Ernest Nolen to A.V. Anderson, June 11, 1919, Inmate File of Ernest Nolen, Inmate Case Files, 7/3/1895–11/5/1957, Records of the Bureau of Prisons, 1870–2009, Record Group 129: Records of the Bureau of Prisons, 1870–2009, National Archives Building, Washington, D.C.

282. "Nolen to Have Bullet Removed After Three Years," *Commercial Appeal* (Memphis, TN), April 2, 1928; "Ernest Nolen Is Better," *Commercial Appeal* (Memphis, TN), May 25, 1928.

283. "Diggs Nolen Isn't Crazy."

284. Ibid.

285. "Past Is Job Bar," *Knoxville (TN) News Sentinel*, August 28, 1928.

Chapter 19

286. "James T. Nolen Dies; Diggs Critically Ill," *Commercial Appeal* (Memphis, TN), September 2, 1928.

287. Ibid.; "Unique Career Ended."

288. "Notorious Man Dies," *Winston County Journal* (Louisville, MS), September 7, 1928.

289. "Nolen Wanted Body Given to University," *Nashville Banner*, (Nashville, TN), September 5, 1928.

290. "James T. Nolen Dies"; "Unique Career Ended"; "50 Years Ago Today," *Commercial Appeal* (Memphis, TN), September 5, 1978.

291. "Unique Career Ended."

292. "Diggs Nolen and Former Wife."

293. "Former Mrs. Nolen Is Sentenced to Prison," *Tennessean* (Nashville, TN), March 13, 1922; "Diggs Nolen Escapes Clutch of Uncle Sam," *Commercial Appeal* (Memphis, TN), December 7, 1923.

294. "Pians and Box Car Mike Face U.S. Hearing Today," *Commercial Appeal* (Memphis, TN), June 18, 1928.

295. "Diggs Nolen Is Dead," *Evening World-Herald*; "Nolen's Brother Says Politicians Aided Diggs Work," *Nashville Tennessean*, September 9, 1928.

296. "Diggs Nolen's Downfall Was Caused by Liquor," *Clarion-Ledger* (Jackson, MS), September 21, 1928.

297. Little, "Hero-Worship."

298. Ibid.

299. "Unique Career Ended."

BIBLIOGRAPHY

Newspapers

Albuquerque (NM) Morning Journal
Arkansas Democrat (Little Rock, AR)
Arkansas Gazette (Little Rock, AR)
Atlanta (GA) Constitution
Baltimore (MD) Sun
Batesville (AR) Guard
Bedford (IN) Daily Mail
Bridgeport (CT) Times and Evening Farmer
Brooklyn Daily Eagle (New York, NY)
Bryan (TX) Daily Eagle and Pilot
Chattanooga (TN) Daily Times
Cherryvale (OK) Weekly Journal
Chicago Tribune
Clarion-Ledger (Jackson, MS)
Columbia (TN) Herald
Covington (TN) Leader
Daily Ardmoreite (Ardmore, OK)
Daily Arkansas Gazette (Little Rock, AR)
Daily News (New York, NY)
Delta-Democrat Times (Greenville, MS)
Deseret News (Salt Lake City, UT)

El Paso (TX) Herald
Evening Times-Republican (Marshalltown, IO)
Gazette (Cedar Rapids, IO)
Hattiesburg (MS) News
Houston (TX) Post
Inter Ocean (Chicago, IL)
Kingfisher (OK) Daily Free Press
Lansing (KS) News
Las Vegas (NV) Optic
Leavenworth (KS) Times
Lexington (TN) Progress
Log Cabin Democrat (Conway, AR)
McNairy County Independent (Selmer, TN)
Morning Tulsa (OK) Daily World
Nashville Tennessean
New York (NY) Herald
New York (NY) Tribune
News Scimitar (Memphis, TN)
North Mississippi Herald (Water Valley, MS)
Omaha (NE) Daily Bee
Ottawa (KS) Daily Republic
Oxford (MS) Eagle
Pensacola (FL) Journal
Pittsburgh (PA) Daily Post
Rock Island Argus (Davenport, IA)
Santa Fe New Mexican
St. Louis (MO) Globe-Democrat
Tennessean (Nashville, TN)
Times-Democrat (New Orleans, LA)
Times-Democrat (Pawnee, OK)
Topeka (KS) State Journal
Tulsa Daily World (OK)
Vicksburg (MS) Evening Post
Winona (MS) Times

Books, Journals and Primary Sources

Bearden, Willie. *100 Years of the Juvenile Court.* 2010. Accessed March 19, 2023. https://vimeo.com/420860628?fbclid=IwAR05FpdSD8IH4MN 6FZ3-dx9yyRUcn9rgh14iKtzemCKiJCjz_pJQnivgQ7I.

Biles, Roger. *Memphis in the Great Depression.* Knoxville: University of Tennessee Press, 1986.

Connelley, William E. *A Standard History of Kansas and Kansans.* Chicago: Lewis, 1918.

Courtwright, David, Herman Joseph and Don Des Jarlais. *Addicts Who Survived: An Oral History of Narcotic Use in America Before 1965.* Knoxville: University of Tennessee Press, 1989.

Dowdy, G. Wayne. *Mayor Crump Don't Like It: Machine Politics in Memphis.* Jackson: University Press of Mississippi, 2006.

Duncan, Martha Grace. "A Strange Liking: Our Admiration for Criminals." *University of Illinois Law Review* no. 1 (1991).

Lauterbach, Preston. *Beale Street Dynasty: Sex, Song, and the Struggle for the Soul of Memphis.* New York: W.W. Norton, 2015.

Lucko, Paul. "Rusk Penitentiary." *Handbook of Texas Online.* Austin, TX: Texas State Historical Association, 2021. Published June 1, 1995; updated January 14, 2021. http://www.tshaonline.org/handbook/ online/articles/jjr01.

Marion, Nancy E., and Willard M. Oliver, eds. *Drugs in American Society*: *An Encyclopedia of History, Politics, Culture, and the Law.* Vol. 2. Santa Barbara, CA: ABC-CLIO, 2015. Accessed via Gale eBooks.

Miller, William D. *Memphis During the Progressive Era, 1900–1917.* Memphis, TN: Memphis State University Press, 1957.

Nolan [*sic*], Ella Brantley. Death certificate. State of Tennessee, State Board of Health, Bureau of Vital Statistics, Certificate of Death, file 1675, May 31, 1923.

Ohio Department of Health, Office of Vital Statistics. Ohio Marriages, 1800–1958, database, *FamilySearch* (https://familysearch.org/ ark:/61903/1:1:XDCZ-11V, December 8, 2014), Henry D. Nolen and Margaret May Haring, 04 Sep 1922; citing, Butler, Ohio, reference 2:3JLJR7N; FHL microfilm 355, 794.

Phillips, Virginia. "Rowlett Paine, Mayor of Memphis, 1919–1924." *West Tennessee Historical Society Papers* 13 (1959).

Rowlett Paine Collection, Memphis Public Library and Information Center, Memphis and Shelby County Room.

Sigafoos, Robert A. *Cotton Row to Beale Street: A Business History of Memphis.* Memphis, TN: Memphis State University Press, 1979.

Speaker, Susan L. "Revealing Data: Collecting Data about TB, Ca. 1900." U.S. National Library of Medicine. National Institutes of Health, January 31, 2018. https://circulatingnow.nlm.nih.gov/2018/01/31/collecting-data-about-tuberculosis-ca-1900/.

Sutch, Richard. "Liberty Bonds." Federal Reserve History. United States Federal Reserve, Washington, D.C., 2015. Accessed March 19, 2023. https://www.federalreservehistory.org/essays/liberty-bonds.

United States Bureau of Prisons. Inmate File of Ernest Nolen, Inmate Case Files, 7/3/1895–11/5/1957, Records of the Bureau of Prisons, 1870–2009, Record Group 129: Records of the Bureau of Prisons, 1870–2009, National Archives Building, Washington, D.C.

———. Inmate Files of Diggs Nolen, 1913–1917 (24726407) [Electronic Record]; Series: Inmate Case Files, 7/3/1895–11/5/1957, Record Group 129: Records of the Bureau of Prisons, 1870–2009; National Archives Building, Washington, D.C.

Watson, Ella Malone. *Walter Malone: Selected Poems.* Louisville, KY: John P. Morton, 1919.

INDEX

P

Paine, J. Rowlett 58, 60, 61, 88, 96, 97, 98, 99
Pantages Theater 90
Patterson, Malcom 89, 100, 110
People's Bank of Collierville robbery 56
Perry, Oliver 29, 31, 59, 61, 72, 76, 77, 78, 79
Pian, Maurice 102
Pinkerton Detective Agency 19, 22, 42
Priddy, R.E. 64, 68
prohibition 61, 77, 110
Pumphrey, Neils Keren "Popeye" 102
Puryear, D.B. 94

Q

Quianthy, Lee 56, 84, 99, 103

R

Rosenberg, Jacob 68, 69
Rosewater, Charles A. (Dr.) 49
Rosser, Helen 42, 44
Ross, John W. (Judge) 88, 94, 98
Rusk Penitentiary, Rusk, Texas 19

S

Smiddy, Will (Det.) 29, 30, 31
Spanish-American War 17, 32, 33

T

Taylor, Neumon (Dr.) 10
Tennessee State Penitentiary 98
train robberies 28
Tri-State Fairgrounds Amusement Park 49
Tulane University 22, 91

U

Utley, R.A. (Commissioner) 32, 33

V

Vanelli, Tony (a.k.a Antonio Santini, the Chief) 66, 67, 68, 70
Van Ray Pharmacy 84
Vardaman, James K. (Senator) 35
Vardaman, James Money 68
Vigilantes (citizens' group) 77, 78
voter registrations 59

W

Wallace, Andy 102
whiskey 60
Wikoff, Ethel 23, 24, 25, 31, 34, 35, 43, 44, 45, 54, 55, 56, 62, 69, 70, 71, 72, 74, 77, 88, 102, 103, 109, 110
shootings 62, 71
Wilkerson and Sons Drug Company 81, 82, 86, 89, 90, 91, 94

ABOUT THE AUTHOR

Patrick O'Daniel is the executive director of library services for Southwest Tennessee Community College in Memphis, Tennessee. He previously worked for the Memphis Public Library and Information Center's History Department, focusing on local history and genealogical collections. He has a master's degree in history from the University of Memphis and a master's degree in library/information sciences from the University of Tennessee, Knoxville. He is the author of *Crusaders, Gangsters, and Whiskey: Prohibition in Memphis* (University Press of Mississippi, 2018), *When the Levee Breaks: Memphis and the Mississippi Valley Flood of 1927* (The History Press, 2013) and *Memphis and the Superflood of 1937* (The History Press, 2010) and coauthor of *Historic Photos of Memphis* (Turner, 2006) with Gina Cordell.